# JACK NICHOLSON

# MOVIE TOP TEN

# CREDITS

**JACK NICHOLSON: MOVIE TOP TEN**
Edited by Mikita Brottman
ISBN 1 871592 98 4
© Creation Books & individual contributors 1999
*Creation Movie Top Tens: a periodical, review-based publication*
First published 2000 by:
**Creation Books International**
*Design/layout/typesetting:*
Bradley Davis, PCP International
*Cover illustration:*
"One Flew Over The Cuckoo's Nest"

*Photo credits:*
All photos are authorized publicity stills, by courtesy of the BFI, London; Kobal Collection, London; MOMA, New York; and the Jack Hunter Collection.

*Copyright acknowledgements:*
Every reasonable effort has been made to trace the owners of copyright materials in this book, but in some instances this has proven impossible. The editor and publishers will be glad to receive information leading to more complete acknowledgements in subsequent printings of the book, and in the meantime extend their apologies for any omissions.

*British Library Cataloguing in Publication Data:*
A catalogue record for this book is available from the British Library

*A Butcherbest Production*

**Creation Books**
*"Popular books for popular people"*

# www.creationbooks.com

# CONTENTS

# INTRODUCTION
# "JACK, KNAVE, JOKER, KING"

Robert Evans calls him the "glittering vagrant"; Pauline Kael describes him a "leering leprechaun"; Peter Thomson calls him an "ebullient lounge lizard"; his current self-styled nickname is "Dr. Devil"; a recent *Newsweek* article describes him as "grinning hedonistically against the moral confusion of our time". Jack Nicholson's appeal is fascinatingly consistent, even in the face of publicity that would seriously damage a lesser star – the press love their intermittent exposés of "spanking Jack", the snickering, sadistic, girl-chasing coke-fiend. But it's too late for any of that to hurt him now – and, after all, such mischievous escapades are part of his public persona as an ironic and flamboyant swinger, Mr. Hollywood, the indispensable joker in the pack. Notorious as a cocky playboy and wicked, exuberant charmer, Jack the Lad is well known as the host of countless cocaine and champagne parties up on Mulholland Drive. At the same time, ironically, this hip rascal is also one of us. This man with an ordinary but endlessly fascinating face is also flawed, childish, egotistical, an ordinary Joe who walks around town without a bodyguard or retinue, who rarely misses a Lakers game, who's generous to a fault with handshakes and autographs. And then there's also "bad Jack", Jack of the rants and tantrums, hell-bent and sinister, Jack of the slitted eyes – an expression he developed for **Prizzi's Honor** (1985) and, as he told interviewers, borrowed from his dog "when he'd just killed another dog". And then, to add yet another level of irony, it's also part of Nicholson's public persona that he's a genius in handling publicity, an arch-manipulator of his own image.

## EARLY DAYS
John Joseph Nicholson Jr. was born in Neptune, New Jersey on April 22 1937, the only son – or so he believed – of John Joseph and Ethel May Nicholson. John Joseph Sr., a window dresser and sign painter, was an alcoholic who abandoned his wife and family soon after the birth of Jackie, as he came to be known. Hardly an auspicious beginning, and yet Mrs. Nicholson was strong and determined, and after her husband left her, started a beauty parlour from a room in the family home and soon developed a thriving business. Jack and his two older sisters – June and Lorraine – moved to a bigger establishment, and young Jackie was able to enjoy a generally stable, middle-class upbringing.

At school, Jack was reputedly bright, funny and gifted. He dabbled in dramatics, played on the basketball team, and had plenty of friends. After a toying for a while with going on the University of Delaware, he gradually began to resist the idea of further schooling and instead, at the age of seventeen, followed his sister June to Los Angeles. Here, he found a job as messenger boy in the cartoon department at MGM for thirty dollars a week. A classic beginning to the career trajectory of the archetypal Hollywood star – except for the fact that Jack had to spend another nineteen years scratching and clawing his way through a catalogue of cheap, forgettable B-movies before audiences could put a name to the face behind that "killer smile".

Jack's journey to self-discovery began in the studio of Jeff Corey, a teacher whose basic theory, in Nicholson's words, was that "you have at least seventy-five per cent in common with any character you'll ever play". Jack began at Jeff Corey's school while he was working in the mail room at MGM – and, as the essays in this book suggest, became increasingly analytical and methodical in his approach to acting. With all his improvisational mystique, easy-going nature and laconic appeal, it's easy to forget that Nicholson is one of the most assiduously trained motion picture stars in the history of Hollywood. It was from Corey that he began to develop his own organizational style, and to learn where he really wanted to go as an actor. He also made a number of close friends in the business – other would-be big-shots including James Coburn, Roger Corman and Robert Towne, colleagues with whom Jack's career continued to link and intertwine for the next fifty years.

But at the beginning, it seemed, to those who knew him, that Jack was just out to have some fun. Most of his first experiences were in small budget television productions and commercials, and he never seemed to have more than a transitory interest in theatre. In fact, most of the people who remember Jack in the fifties recall that his interest was less in the work than for the lifestyle of contemporary Hollywood – a bohemian sideshow in a process of fascinating upheaval. His attitude changed in the sixties and seventies when the projects he was offered became increasingly substantial, but in the fifties, Nicholson's interest in acting seemed more social than professional. He hung out in the circles around James Dean and Marlon Brando, with beatniks and hippy philosophers, smoked a lot of marijuana, and studied the Method as a license for self-indulgent behaviour and wild experiments rather than a form of dramatic expression. He shared a cluttered apartment on the borders of Hollywood with Robert Towne, drank at the Raincheck Room on Sunset, was always on the fringes of the centre, hanging out, getting into fights and chasing girls rather than working his way assiduously up the ladder of opportunity, like some of his more serious colleagues.

Many people commented that the Jack of the early Hollywood days was a character who seemed to lack intensity, who would smile, do impressions, tell jokes and generally hang around on the fringes of the interesting scenes, but never made much of an impact, either personally or professionally. There seems to have been very little early indication of his latent potential as an actor – in fact, Jeff Corey made a note in his files about Nicholson that read "Consider terminating for lack of interest" (Shepherd, 31). John Gilmore remembers Nicholson as an awkward hanger-on. "If we were discussing something that we considered heavy about acting", recalls Gilmore, "Jack would just disconnect. After a while he'd get up and wander off, disappear. I don't care who claims now to have seen potential in him, the fact is, no-one took him seriously then" (Gilmore, cit in Shepherd, 30).

## THE CORMAN YEARS

Roger Corman had been producing low-budget B-movies long before he joined Jeff Corey's acting class, which he entered mainly to meet acting students who he could employ cheaply in his second-billed cheapies. In 1957, Corman offered Nicholson the starring role as a tough but lovelorn teenager in the summer drive-in quickie, **The Cry Baby Killer**. Jack gave a solid performance which won favourable comments from a couple of critics, but his "big break" in the movies was hardly a momentous one, and it was two years before he starred in another film, playing the part of a masochistic dental patient in **The Little Shop Of Horrors**. In 1960 he had small roles in Corman's **The Wild Ride** and Irving Lerner's **Studs Lonigan**.

In all these productions, Nicholson proved himself capable of a diverse range of characters, but none of his roles were especially remarkable, mainly because Corman's aim was to make movies as quickly and as cheaply as possible. Typical of Corman's work was his 1963 production **The Raven**, in which Nicholson was cast as the son of Peter Lorre, and when the movie was completed two days ahead of schedule, Corman decided to knock off another film on the same sets, which led to the ill-conceived absurdity, **The Terror**. Starring alongside Jack in **The Terror** was his first wife, Sandra Knight, whom he married in 1961. Despite the tackiness of this film, however, it "helped initiate a whole new cycle of horror films and a new kind of true-to-life monster which was to replace the 'painted monsters' of Karloff's generation", as Ruth Goldberg explains in her essay herein.

Frustrated by the way he seemed to be struggling along from picture to picture, Nicholson next decided to try his hand at some behind-the-scenes work – writing, producing and directing. With a little help from an old friend Don Devlin, he wrote a screenplay for the B-movie **Thunder Island** in 1963, then teamed up with provocative director Monte Hellman to work on two action-quickies made in the Philippines, **Back Door To Hell** in 1964, and **Flight To Fury** two years later. On the basis of these two films – both of which were commercially successful and got reasonably good reviews – Roger Corman gave Hellman and Nicholson the backing to produce two westerns,

**The Shooting** and **Ride In The Whirlwind**, both made in 1966. Totally uncommercial – at least, for the American market – Jack referred to this pair of elusive movies as "existential Westerns", and touted them around the European film festivals, where they won a certain amount of success, especially in France. Ironically, these were the first films that Jack really felt proud of, but they were considered too offbeat and "philosophical" for American audiences, and were withheld from U.S. release until 1972, when Nicholson had established himself as a major Hollywood player.

Jack always liked to smoke pot, and in the mid-sixties a psychiatrist friend turned him on the LSD as part of an experiment in regression. From this and other colourful experiences – including his divorce from Sandra Knight – came Nicholson's three drug movies of the late sixties, **The Trip**, **Head** and **Psych-Out**. **The Trip**, directed by Roger Corman, starred Peter Fonda, Susan Strasberg and Dennis Hopper. Nicholson wrote the script, based on his own psychedelic experiences, since, he claimed, Corman "didn't have as much experience with LSD as I did" – though he later complained that Roger deleted a lot of his best material (Siegel, 36). Nevertheless, **The Trip** was a huge commercial success, and Nicholson was rewarded with the lead role in AIP's 1968 LSD vehicle **Psych-Out**, a curious experiment in hazy, psychedelic special effects. In 1968, Jack teamed up with pals Bob Rafelson and Bert Schneider to produce **Head**, yet another homage to psychedelics, this time featuring The Monkees and Frank Zappa. If none of these films brought Jack much public attention at the time, they certainly had a significant impact on his career, by hooking him up with a number of important future collaborators, namely Bob Rafelson and Bert Schneider, as well as Peter Fonda and Dennis Hopper. It was this period which also saw Jack involved in the first wave of biker movies, appearing in **Hell's Angels On Wheels** and **The Rebel Rousers**, as well as the seminal biker/road epic, **Easy Rider**.

## EASY RIDER

**Easy Rider** grew out of the working relationship that developed between Fonda and Hopper while they were working together on **The Trip**. They employed novelist Terry Southern to help them work on an idea they'd had about two bikers who made a lot of money selling cocaine and used it to ride their bikes east in search of America. The screenplay went through a number of changes involving various collaborators, and was shipped around from Columbia to AIP and back again. Tales of the shoot itself are legendary, generally involving plenty of rock music, LSD, motorbikes, parties, self-indulgence and an inexhaustible supply of drugs and film stock. Jack was enlisted by Bert Schneider to play straight-laced but disillusioned alcoholic Southern lawyer George Hanson, after Rip Torn had grown disillusioned with

**Easy Rider**

the chaotic atmosphere on set. Jack was originally sent down to help bring some stability and responsibility to the proceedings, but ended up as a main player in the anarchy which was to finally establish his screen presence.

And what a presence. In the role of Hanson, Jack allegedly modelled his Texas accent on that of President Lyndon Johnson, and also drew upon the figure of his alcoholic grandfather – wearing glasses, for example, exactly like his grandfather wore (Shepherd, 69). He is, by turns, odd and engaging, creepy and comical, melancholic and maniacal. In essence, George Hanson contains all the elements of what was to become the quintessential Jack Nicholson persona: self-conscious, wryly cynical, stylishly grotesque. Though the film itself now seems slightly choppy and dated, Jack's performance still stands out as the best of the movie. **Easy Rider** was named Best Film at the

Cannes Film Festival of 1969, and Jack was nominated for a Supporting Actor Award at the 1969 Oscars. At 32 years old, he was finally a star.

## THE SEVENTIES

After the success of **Easy Rider**, Jack found himself able to call the shots for the first time in his life. In 1970 he directed **Drive, He Said**, based on the novel by Jeremy Larner – a movie which took advantage of Jack's knowledge of basketball, his devotion to the L.A. Lakers, and his radical politics. The film was savaged by the critics and condemned by the censors for its controversial scenes of nudity and profane language, and Jack was reputedly exhausted by the experience, and very depressed at its failure (Siegel, 49). And yet the failure of **Drive, He Said** was quickly overshadowed by the success of his next project, **Five Easy Pieces**.

In **Five Easy Pieces**, Jack began to show a more inspired and thoughtful style of acting. As Bobby Dupea, Nicholson plays a middle-class intellectual who drops out, only to realize that the alternative lifestyle isn't all it's cracked up to be. Like Jack's next film **Carnal Knowledge**, **Five Easy Pieces** won rave reviews. In these seminal films of the early seventies, Nicholson attains a new lean and muscular style of acting, which relates directly to the influence of Jeff Corey's studio and the precision and spareness of Rafelson's directing. In this volume, Colin Gardner examines how, in this film, Jack begins to experiment with his own screen identity by working against the sixties version of the countercultural male, negotiating new ways of dealing with conventional expectations of gender roles.

Both **Five Easy Pieces** and **Carnal Knowledge** allowed Jack to showcase his increasing range of acting talents, which thrillingly complemented the irresponsible sense of hedonism that seemed constantly to be lurking behind the shadow of that lethal grin. When Nicholson was nominated for the Best Actor Oscar for his part in **Five Easy Pieces**, *Time* magazine commented that "the role allowed Nicholson not only to turn on his own bursting temper but to flash the charm that has its greatest single emblem in its smile". Significantly, the character of Bobby Dupea – written by Nicholson's old friend Carol Eastman – was based partly on Nicholson himself. His role in **Carnal Knowledge** was a more stoical one, revealing his fascinating ability to diversify by casting him as an outspoken man racked by sexual needs and frustrations, and tormented by private failure. Jack began to be known as one of the finest American screen actors of the seventies.

This reputation was enhanced with the 1972 release of **The King Of Marvin Gardens**, another Bob Rafelson film featuring Nicholson and his friend Bruce Dern as a pair of brothers who get involved in a small-time but grandiose hustle. Upon its release, the film was hardly noticed, but has since been reappropriated as critically significant, especially in the way it allows Jack

to play against the grain as an introverted intellectual. The psychological realism of the way Jack negotiates the tricky dynamic with his brother was repeated in Hal Ashby's 1973 film, **The Last Detail**. For his flawlessly authentic portrait of a career sailor, Nicholson was granted the Best Actor Award at Cannes.

The following years saw Jack really enhance his dramatic reputation and finally come into his own as one of the giants of American film. And as his prestige as an actor increased, so did press interest in his family, his love life, his illegitimate children, his famously short temper and his playboy hi-jinks. After his divorce from Sandra Knight, he was associated with a string of glamorous women – Mimi Machu, Michelle Phillips, Candice Bergen, Margaret Trudeau, Susan Anspach, Brooke Hayward, Karen Black, Joni Mitchell, Faye Dunaway, and finally – though not consistently – Anjelica Huston. And it was in 1974 that Jack learned the devastating news – ironically, from a research reporter for *Time* magazine – that June Nicholson, the woman he'd believed for thirty-seven years to be his older sister, was, in fact, his natural mother. It was another decade, however, before this disturbing family secret was made public.

Not long after Jack's first meeting with Anjelica Huston, he was cast in the starring role of J.J. Gittes in Roman Polanski's 1974 film **Chinatown**, in which Anjelica's famous father, John Huston, played the villain, Noah Cross. Initially the role of Gittes didn't seem to suit Nicholson; the role was that of a romantic leading man, and Jack was more of a character star. As Philip Simpson explains in this volume, however, Jack re-examined and "emasculated" the traditional routine of the hard-boiled private dick, and yet does so without losing his defiant allure. His spectacularly laconic, gritty and bleak performance teamed with an ingenious script by Robert Towne and Polanski's thoughtful direction led **Chinatown** to draw a larger audience than any of Jack's previous films, proving to be an immense critical and financial success. As a romantic leading man, Nicholson had proved he could be a major box office draw.

Other notable films of the seventies include **The Fortune** (Mike Nichols, 1974), **Tommy** (Ken Russell, 1975), **The Missouri Breaks** (Robert Sherman, 1976), **The Last Tycoon** (Elia Kazan, 1976), **Goin' South** (Nicholson, 1978) and, in particular, **The Passenger** (1975) which gave Jack the chance with Michelangelo Antonioni and star in his first European "art movie". But it was for his role as Randle Patrick McMurphy in Milos Forman's **One Flew Over The Cuckoo's Nest** (1975) that Nicholson won his first Best Actor Oscar. As McMurphy, Jack proves craftily endearing in the role of an inmate who cons his way into a psychiatric hospital and becomes known as the inmates' champion. A virtuoso performance – and still perhaps his most memorable – the role of McMurphy not only demonstrated Jack's tremendous

acting range, but also revealed his constant willingness to tackle unexpected projects and take difficult chances. At once playful and sinister, terrifying and hilarious, the portrayal of McMurphy is considered by many critics to be Nicholson's most lasting and significant achievement.

## THE EIGHTIES

Nicholson began the eighties busy at Elstree Studios in North London working on Stanley Kubrick's **The Shining**, co-starring Shelley Duvall and Scatman Crothers. The film was a change of pace for Jack, and – in keeping with his willingness to constantly vary his roles – allowed him to move beyond the constraints of a naturalistic style of acting. As the pathological family man Jack Torrance, Nicholson is a stylised horror-show ogre with a lunatic's rictus. The film was enormously popular at home and abroad, and made a great deal of money.

Whilst some critics accused Jack of histrionics and hammy acting, others believe that this movie contains Nicholson's performative *tour de force*. **The Shining** also marks a move in Nicholson's career away from the "sidewalk naturalism" of the seventies and towards the fantastic, the grotesque, the imaginative and the theatrical. Moreover, whilst in the sixties and seventies Nicholson had often played the part of the rebellious, obstinate, alienated son or brother, the older Jack of the eighties began to take on the role of the frustrated, defective middle-aged male like Jack Torrance, the blundering father-figure in the midst of tormenting self-examination, his characters often undergoing break-up or divorce. Jack does the male mid-life crisis better than anybody else on screen, excelling in roles that take him – as his life seems to have done – from antic renegade to a more fraught, anxious, self-reflective style of masculinity.

Next Nicholson teamed up with old friend Bob Rafelson to make **The Postman Always Rings Twice**, a remake of the Tay Garnett-directed 1946 adaptation of the 1934 James M. Cain novel that had starred Lana Turner and John Garfield. In this Depression-era tale of obsessive lust, Jack interprets the role of the protagonist as that of an aggressive sadist who solution to every problem he encounters is either sex or violence. **Postman** allowed Jack to be sexy in a way audiences hadn't seen before, and whilst the film wasn't a great success in the U.S. – perhaps appearing too controversial for the notoriously strait-laced American audience – it became a major worldwide hit.

In 1981 Nicholson starred in an all-action movie, **The Border**. The film was not a success, and, for the first time, it seemed like Jack's star might have begun to fade. Audiences seemed less interested in him; he seemed to be reaching a significant crossroads, both in his screen career and in his personal life. In the same year as he made **The Border**, Jack took a supporting role in his pal Warren Beatty's *magnum opus*, **Reds**; the film was a personal success for Beatty and Nicholson, but wasn't a big enough hit to immediately earn back its colossal outlay.

His comeback came with the enormous success of the 1983 film **Terms Of Endearment**, directed by James L. Brooks and based on Larry McMurtry's novel about a mother-daughter relationship spanning three decades. Jack was a powerhouse in another supporting role, this time as the paunchy middle-aged playboy and former astronaut Garrett Breedlove. The part could have been written expressly for him, and he played it with a impressive dynamism, charm, surprising humility and occasional trademark pantomimed grimace. In **Terms Of Endearment**, the aging Jack plays a role not too dissimilar from the off-screen Nicholson of the eighties – a male celebrity kicking out against the encroaching pressures of obligation and domestic commitment. Garrett Breedlove finds it difficult to grow out of his carefree playboy lifestyle, despite moments of existential *angst*, waning virility and waxing paunch. Interestingly, Nicholson's particular model of masculinity has seemed constantly potent and appealing, particularly to males (Patrick McGilligan describes him as "a cultural *alter ego* for men").

**Terms Of Endearment** was named Best Picture at that year's Academy Awards, and Jack was named Best Supporting Actor – an award he'd been coveting since he was nominated for his role in **Easy Rider** almost fifteen years before. The success of **Terms** was followed up in 1985 with the bleak, cynical black comedy **Prizzi's Honor**, in which Jack played the role of the flat, cold, brutishly cunning Italian American hit man Charley Pantanna. For her performance as his female counterpart, Jack's girlfriend Anjelica Huston won the Academy Award for Best Supporting Actress, setting a record of three generations of Oscar winners in one family.

More great performances followed. In **Heartburn** (Mike Nichols, 1986), Jack played opposite his idol Meryl Streep in the role of Mark, a philandering husband who wrecks his marriage by cheating on his wife during her pregnancy. The part was based on the character of Watergate journalist Carl Bernstein, but Jack – who knew Bernstein – tried to make his role as different from the reality as possible. He made Mark into a vulnerable, flawed, rather likeable person, a development which – according to some critics, at least – was something of a misjudgement, taking away the abrasive edge that the story needed, and losing some of the sympathy for the character of Rachel (Meryl Streep).

In **The Witches Of Eastwick** (George Miller, 1987), Jack played Darryl Van Horne, a satanic visitor to a small New England town, who causes three of the town's most attractive women (Susan Sarandon, Michelle Pfeiffer and Cher) to abandon themselves to him sexually, causing all kinds of comic chaos to result. The part allowed Jack to indulge in the broader, more exaggerated comic style he'd used earlier in **The Shining**. At first, however, Miller didn't want to cast Nicholson in the role. "My first instinct was: in getting someone for the Devil, you need an actor who is totally unlike the Devil, and Jack clearly has an impish quality", he recalls. "Then, I realised he's like a two hundred year old child: very wise in many ways – even beyond his years – but with a certain innocence and naiveté we expect from someone younger. The moment I saw that, I knew he was the only actor to bring a humanity to the role, to pull the Devil out of stereotype" (cit in Brode, 253). Unsurprisingly, the film was a box-office hit.

In **The Witches Of Eastwick**, Jack negotiates an increasingly self-conscious version of male egotism more appropriate to the transitional period of the eighties, in which Nicholson seemed compelled to pursue his growing fascination with macho and diabolical characters. Perhaps, as John Kimsey suggests in this volume, Jack's fascination with such roles may have something to do with the fact that they allow him to have it both ways – to flaunt his masculinity while broadly poking fun at his misogynistic persona, just as **The Witches Of Eastwick** "privileges the male lead even as it dramatizes his rejection by the women", as Kimsey puts it.

In the same year that **Witches** was released, Jack played a cameo role in James L. Brooks's **Broadcast News**, and won critical acclaim for his portrayal of alcoholic drifter Francis Phelan in Hector Babenco's **Ironweed**, again playing opposite Meryl Streep. However, his most successful role of the eighties – at least financially – was his grotesque rendition of The Joker in Tim Burton's enormous hit, **Batman** (1989). With his shamelessly flamboyant performance – all white hair, green face, fiendish stunts and permanently etched grin – Jack, looking for all the world like a macabre circus clown – was the star of the show.

The Joker is the apotheosis of Jack's demoniac figures – and, significantly, a role which links Nicholson right back to the fifties and sixties and the exaggerated, grotesque characters in the DC comics he used to collect as a boy in New Jersey. As Andrew Adamides rightly observes here, **Batman** unites the retro flavour of such gory and fantastical widely-drawn villains with the astute, market conscious commercialism of the eighties hi-tech blockbuster. This was a part that put no obstacles in the way of Jack's most broad and extravagant acting style. "You couldn't go over the top in that part", commented Jack. "There was no top". The killer smile had never been put to better use.

## THE NINETIES

The last decade has seen Jack maintain his remarkably prolific output, often appearing in two or three films each year, many of them significant box office hits – not least because of the presence of Nicholson himself. In 1992, for example, he appeared as the imperious Nathan R. Jessup, a military

Wolf

"untouchable", in Rob Reiner's blockbuster drama of marines accused of murder, **A Few Good Men**. He also starred opposite Ellen Barkin as a guard dog trainer who gets involved with one of his clients in **Man Trouble** – a rare flop for the generally surefire combination of Bob Rafelson and Carol Eastman. In the same year, Nicholson also starred in **Hoffa**, directed by Danny de Vito from a script by David Mamet. This disappointing film featured Nicholson as legendary union leader Jimmy Hoffa, as seen through the eyes of his friend Bobby Ciaro (De Vito). The film follows Hoffa through countless battles with the RTA and President Roosevelt, and concludes by negating the theory that Hoffa disappeared in 1975. Something of a failure, **Hoffa** was generally condemned as "a bad movie about a bad man".

These two disappointments, however, were more than redeemed by

Nicholson's clever and spirited portrayal of a sensitive, emotional and passionate werewolf in Mike Nichols 1994 box office smash, **Wolf**. Jack was at his fearless best playing opposite Michelle Pfeiffer as publisher Wilf Randall, who has to struggle to save his job from the machinations of archetypal evil yuppie James Spader. His performance in 1995's **The Crossing Guard**, though equally absorbing, could not be more different in style and tone. As Tony Williams explains here, Jack's role in Sean Penn's critically acclaimed dark and seedy drama brings us an older and wiser Nicholson, though one who still resists clichés.

In this emotionally tense drama, Nicholson gives a thrillingly authentic performance as seedy jeweller Freddy Gale, a man who's sworn to kill the drunk driver who took the life of his little girl. Though Gale is often sleazy and unlikeable, Jack never loses audience sympathy, and seems to capture the spirit of the weaselly Freddy from the inside out. As Williams points out, **The Crossing Guard** sees Jack returning to his earlier mode of naturalism and rediscovering his subtle, nuanced performative style of the seventies, now enhanced by the authority gained from a life lived in the gaze of an eager and envious public.

In 1996, Jack returned in a cameo role as Garrett Breedlove in Robert Harling's moderately successful follow-up to **Terms Of Endearment**, **The Evening Star**. By far his greatest performance of that year, however, was as President Dale in Tim Burton's zany alien invasion spoof, **Mars Attacks!**. Nicholson plays all-out crazy in this manically cynical special-effects extravaganza, full of talented stars – and also featuring Welsh singer Tom Jones. In his psychotic portrayal of a deranged U.S. President, Jack looks like he's enjoying every second of this wild, demented spoof.

The following year saw him team up with Michael Caine in another Bob Rafelson-directed movie, the heist drama **Blood And Wine**. According to Rafelson, **Blood And Wine** was the final part of a trilogy that began with **Five Easy Pieces** and continued with **The King Of Marvin Gardens**, in which Jack played the parts of son and brother respectively. In **Blood And Wine** he plays the part of a dismal father, Alex, a wealthy wine dealer who – over the years – has distanced himself from his wife and son through his negligence and philandering. The film garnered mixed reviews, though Jack's creepy performance as Alex was singled out as especially vital and well-observed.

The same year, Jack starred in another James L. Brooks feature, the enormously successful **As Good As It Gets**, a warm, fresh, vivacious character-driven comedy. **As Good As It Gets** explores the complex dynamic of shifting relationships between a gay artist (Greg Kinnear), a single mother/waitress (Helen Hunt), and a cranky, bigoted, obsessive-compulsive writer (Nicholson). Jack's characteristically authentic, original and emotionally

23

complex performance was rewarded with another well-deserved Best Actor Academy Award.

And, at the age of sixty-three, Jack Nicholson goes from strength to strength, showing no sign of relenting from his remarkably productive schedule. He's currently working on another movie directed by Sean Penn, whose working title is **The Pledge**, in which he plans to take a supporting role alongside such thespian luminaries as Vanessa Redgrave and Helen Mirren. Clearly, after five decades on the screen, his initial enthusiasm never seems to have diminished. "Nicholson, who is one of the world's greatest actors... is like a force of nature", writes cinematographer Nestor Almendros, who worked with Jack on the western **Goin' South** (1978). "Working with him is both stimulating and difficult, but his enthusiasm is contagious; it sweeps the crew along like a cyclone".

Of the current select circle of Hollywood greats – Hoffman, Brando, Redford, Pacino, De Niro – Jack Nicholson is the only one we really feel we *know*. Perhaps this is because his characters always seem to somehow draw their essence from the off-screen life of the actor himself ("my secret craft – it's all autobiography", claimed Nicholson in a 1986 interview in *American Film*) – and yet, ironically, each of his performances is usually vastly different from the next. Perhaps it's because – unlike his reclusive neighbour, Marlon Brando – Nicholson is simply so *present*, so much a part of the current Hollywood scene, whether cheering on the Lakers, crashing his car on Sunset Boulevard, hanging out on the slopes at Aspen or mooning Celtic fans at Boston Garden. Perhaps it's because he consistently refuses to play the game of oozing "character" and "sincerity" on sleazy and sanctimonious television talkshows.

Or perhaps it's because he seems so quintessentially a man of our times, a man who grew up in the fifties, was formed and molded by the sixties, remained cheerfully unreconstructed throughout the seventies and eighties and now, at the turn of the century, has achieved the status of Great Man. The films analyzed in this volume chart an engaging cross-section of a career that seems, in its style, sensibility and choice of roles, to shape the inner history of contemporary America.

**Works Cited**

Braithwaite, Bruce, *The Films Of Jack Nicholson*, BCW Publishing, London 1977.
Brode, Douglas, *The Films Of Jack Nicholson*, Secaucus, Citadel Press, NJ 1987.
Crane, Richard David, and Christopher Fryer, *Jack Nicholson: Face To Face*, M. Evans, NY 1975.
Dickens, Norman, *Jack Nicholson: The Search For A Superstar*, Signet, London & NY 1975.
Downing, David, *Jack Nicholson*, Stein and Day, NY 1984.
Shepherd, Donald, *Jack Nicholson*, Thomas Dunne, NY 1991.
Siegel, Barbara and Scott, *Jack Nicholson: The Unauthorised Biography*, Angus & Robertson, London 1990.

# THE REMAINS OF A ONCE NOBLE HOUSE: FREUD'S FAMILY ROMANCE IN 'THE TERROR'

*They don't make movies like **The Terror** any more.*[1]
—Jack Nicholson

Why take a fresh look at **The Terror**? Long since written off as a Roger Corman in-joke, the movie has been alternately lampooned and savaged by filmmakers and critics for generations. Film scholars gleefully pan the film all over again every few years as new books emerge on the works of Nicholson, Karloff, Coppola and Corman, calling it "faux Poe"[2], "a legendary mess"[3], and even comparing it to week-old leftovers from a Thanksgiving dinner.[4]

In the past, scholars of "serious" film have ignored movies like **The Terror**, made outside the mainstream and eliminated from consideration by virtue of low budget and "low culture" status. In recent years, however, low budget, independent films have begun to receive overdue critical acclaim, and "schlock" films are being re-examined, under the premise that "bad" films, and bad horror films in particular, can often be unexpectedly effective. The viewer, not anticipating any emotional interaction with the movie, leaves his/her conscious defenses down in a way that allows the movie to get under the skin, undetected.[5]

Up until now there has been a general agreement that the plot of **The Terror** doesn't make any sense and that Nicholson "looks lost"[6] in his role (an odd criticism, considering that his character in the film is, quite literally, lost in a strange land). Historians have played up the dubious origins of the film, calling it the shoddiest of the Corman quickies: shot in three days, without a script, to wring one last performance out of Boris Karloff's contract, and to utilize the sets from Corman's previous movie **The Raven** (also 1963) as they were being torn down, **The Terror** was a last minute endeavour which then dragged on for months as Corman hired one director after another to shoot and splice in additional footage, in the hopes of creating a coherent story.

Corman's work during this period strongly reflects the influence of psychoanalysis. By his own account, he'd entered into Freudian analysis at this time, and was exploring the relationship between horror and Freud's concept of the unconscious. This process is nowhere more apparent than in **The Terror**: unable to accept that his "Poe cycle" (during which he made eight films based on the writings of Edgar Allan Poe in four years, and which has been hailed as his finest work[7]) was coming to a close, Corman grabbed a camera and in an innovative and unorthodox way, produced what is, in essence, a free-associative film, playing off his relationship with Poe's work. In his own words:

*I felt that Poe and Freud had been working in different ways toward a concept of the unconscious mind, so I tried to use Freud's theories to interpret the work of Poe... I was getting so familiar with the standard elements of Poe's material... that I tried to out-Poe Poe himself and create a gothic tale from scratch. In fact* **The Terror** *began as a challenge: to shoot most of a gothic horror film in two days, using leftover sets from* **The Raven**. *It turned into the longest production of my career – an ordeal that required five directors and nine months to complete. But... it's a classic story of how to make a film out of nothing... We had a roughed-out story line but no one really knew what their characters' motivations were because we didn't exactly know what was supposed to happen to them. But I kept shooting. I told my d.p. 'Don't slate the shots. We'll worry later what to do with this film. We'll just start and stop the camera for now.' 'I've never heard of anything like this in my entire career' he said. Of course he hadn't. No one had. Everybody got into the spirit and laughed.*[8]

The plot took numerous twists over the following months, and ultimately became so confusing that, in the end, a scene had to be added in which one character turns to another and explains what's going on in the narrative. Lapses in continuity aside, Corman's familiarity with Poe's gloomy gothic atmosphere is indeed evident in the film. Many of Poe's most significant images appear in **The Terror**, and the film is strengthened by their (potentially) symbolic resonance for the audience. The plot, for example, primarily unfolds in a gothic castle overlooking the sea. This immediately sets the stage for the viewer to experience the action of the film as an interior drama. If "the castle" in Poe's work is often interpreted as a metaphor for the conscious mind ("The palace is an elaborate conceit for the human mind – the place where consciousness dwells[9]"), then the image of the sea below lends itself to a metaphor for the unconscious. True to Poe's vision, the boundaries between conscious and unconscious (as well as sea and castle) are ultimately obscured in the film.

    Film and psychoanalytic theory usually overlap only in academic circles, and then usually in reference to "art films" or acknowledged "classics". But it seems as though **The Terror**, with its many disjunctures and irrational twists, only really comes alive when analyzed as one might examine a dream. Seen from this standpoint, its weaknesses become strengths, and Nicholson's performance surely deserves a second look.

## GHOSTS OF PAST GLORY

André Duvalier (Jack Nicholson), a Napoleonic soldier returning from the wars, is lost somewhere along the Baltic coast. The sun beats down on him and he's weak from thirst. His compass is revealed to be broken, a sign to the experienced viewer of horror film that the traveller has entered the realm of the uncanny, "not on any map".[10] The young man falls from his horse in a dead faint and is awakened some time later by the incoming tide washing over his body.

A lovely, silent young woman (Hélène, played by Sandra Knight – Nicholson's first wife) appears out of nowhere and leads the soldier to fresh water. The two young people experience an instant chemistry, but the ghostly beauty leads the soldier out into the surf only to disappear suddenly as a raven swoops down and viciously attacks the young man, causing him to once again lose consciousness and sink beneath the waves. He sees Hélène's face in his dreams, but the image transforms into that of an old crone (Dorothy Neumann) standing over him as he regains consciousness in a hut in the woods. A raven sits in a cage nearby. When the soldier inquires about the young woman, the crone vehemently denies her existence, telling him that "Hélène" is merely the bird's name and assuring him that the encounter was a delusion. André is left unsure about what he has seen.

That night as André wanders into the forest, the woman, Hélène, appears to him again and asks him to follow her. Gustav, (Jackie Haze) the old woman's mute servant, appears just in time to prevent André from following the apparition into a patch of quicksand, as Hélène disappears into the mist. This is the second time she has almost led him to his death. The mute (who apparently can speak, albeit in a whisper) tells the shocked young man "She knows not what she does. Her will is not her own... Possessed!" He instructs André to go to a nearby castle where he may uncover the truth behind Hélène's mysterious existence, and hints only that the secret involves "Eric".

In the morning the old woman is eager to get rid of him, but becomes frightened when André tells her his intention to go to the castle in search of answers, and urges him not to go. "These are things beyond your understanding", she adds, cryptically. Undaunted, however, André resumes his search, and narrowly escapes being crushed by a sudden and inexplicable avalanche of falling rocks. At the castle, he is met by the Baron von Leppe (Boris Karloff), who informs him that the apparition André has seen is not a living woman but the ghost of the baron's wife, Ilsa, who's been dead for twenty years.

Unable to accept this fantastic turn of events, Duvalier decides to stay

at the castle, where he is distinctly unwelcome, until he can determine whether Ilsa/Hélène is indeed a ghost. All manner of eerie disturbances occur in the dark castle as night falls: candles suddenly blow out, creaking doors lock and unlock themselves without human assistance, there are distant, unearthly screams and rattles in the night. From a distance André sees the ghostly figure of Hélène appear and disappear once more into the darkness. In the morning, Stephan, the Baron's faithful servant (Dick Miller) urges the Baron to send André away, afraid that the young man may uncover a secret they are eager to keep hidden. André confronts the Baron: "You're anxious to be rid of me – are you afraid I might find out about Eric?"

Consequently, the Baron confesses that twenty years earlier he killed his wife in a jealous rage, while Stephan disposed of her lover, Eric. No one was ever told the true cause of the baroness's death, and the Baron's self-imposed penance for the sin of murder has been confinement within the castle walls from that day forward, haunted by the ghost of Ilsa. Nearby, Gustav the mute finds Hélène gazing dreamily out to sea, as if in a trance. He urges her to disobey the old woman and return to the place from which she was summoned. "Only when the sea enters the crypt," she replies. The raven appears overhead, and, as if speaking through her, Hélène translates its words for Gustav: "The old one calls. She warns you Gustav, she will be patient with you no longer."

In the forest, Stephan spies on the old woman performing an act of black magic, channelling a ghost into Hélène's body: "Hélène, be as though you never were. Spirit of Ilsa, speak through her and do my bidding. Soon you will have the strength to carry out my vengeance." Meanwhile, back at the castle, the Baron finally loses his temper and orders André to leave. As he rides away, Gustav appears in his path, but the raven swoops down out of the sky attacking Gustav and ripping his eyes out before he can speak. As he dies, Gustav implores André to go back and help Hélène.

Arriving back at the castle, André finds Hélène unwilling to leave with him, for she "is possessed of the dead" and can only leave once the sea enters the crypt beneath the castle. André insists that there are doctors in Paris who can cure her of this delusion, but she abruptly disappears once more. Following her into the crypt André is shocked by a hazy vision of Ilsa/Hélène entreating the Baron to take his own life so that they may rest together in the tomb for eternity. The Baron is in agony, fearing that his soul will be damned for the sin of suicide. André bursts in. "Let me see who you really are! What kind of woman are you?" he demands, as the apparition vanishes through the locked door to the crypt.

Investigating a mysterious light in the room that belonged to the late Baroness, André and Stephan find a cradle next to the bed. "Did the Baroness have a child?" asks André. "I never knew of it," replies Stephan. Suddenly the Baron appears in a rage at the intrusion. "You spare me nothing!" he cries, and orders André to leave once more. As Stephan escorts him out at gunpoint they encounter the old witch who cackles that her hour of vengeance on the Baron is at hand. For what offense? "He killed my son – Eric."

At this point André turns to Stephan and explains "She used the girl as a puppet to drive the Baron to suicide. She didn't know that it was you who killed Eric." Stephan breaks down and confesses that the story of Eric's death has been an elaborate lie. "In the struggle", he confesses, "it was the Baron who was killed, not Eric. And Eric took his place without anyone ever knowing. But he took his place in mind as well as body. In his mind, Eric is the Baron von Leppe." The witch, realizing she has driven her own son to suicide tries to enter the crypt, but bursts into flames on the threshold of the adjoining chapel. Down in the crypt, Eric/the Baron has opened the floodgates to the sea and is waist deep in water when the possessed Hélène appears to taunt him, assuring him that his soul will indeed suffer eternal damnation.

The Baron tries to close the gates but it is too late – he's pulled under by the current as André arrives just in time to pull Hélène to safety. He kisses her passionately and then recoils in horror as she turns into a rotting corpse before his very eyes. Could she have been the Baron's dead wife after all?

## THE RETURN OF THE REPRESSED
*"The Uncanny is... everything that ought to have remained secret and hidden, but has come to light."*
—Sigmund Freud[11]

As the protagonist in this nightmare, Nicholson does well to look lost. The dream disorients him at every turn – an overwhelming and overdetermined drama of ambivalence, generational conflict and sexual repression. If a dream is a wish in disguise, as Freud would have it, then the wish this dream explores is so disturbing and taboo to the dreamer that it has been transformed into a morass of contradictory desires. Ambivalence, in dreams, is often expressed by "doubling": two characters who emerge in opposition to one another, each embodying one side of the conflict. In **The Terror** there are six characters, which divide logically into three pairs of doubles. Each pair clearly embodies a conflict in the cinematic dream.

The old baron haunted by a guilty secret finds his double in the form of the young officer of the French revolution who comes to expose it. The servant who would die to protect the secret is doubled by another who does die trying to bring it to light. And the embittered old hag who wants revenge is doubled by the young, innocent beauty possessed by a force out of the past.[12]

Repression, according to Freud, protects people from facing their most unsettling inner desires head on[13]. In this cinematic nightmare, confronting the "secret" or repressed material would be so devastating to the dreamer that almost all of the action revolves around preventing this from happening. Everyone keeps telling André to leave before its too late, not to believe what he has seen, and not to meddle in "things beyond his understanding."

These warnings don't just come from the other characters, moreover. The elements conspire against André as well: he's almost drowned, crushed by an avalanche and enveloped in quicksand in the first fifteen minutes of the film in various attempts to keep him from reaching his destination. Only "the return of the repressed", the powerful force which turns dreams into nightmares, can override such consistent warnings. It's as if the secret has taken on a destructive power all its own, and must come to light at any cost. Once repression is released there's no harnessing it again, and this idea is vividly represented by the image of the Baron trying to hold back the sea after opening the castle gates. According to Corman:

*I was also using what I knew of Freud's dream interpretations and my own analysis to make the picture[14] work on an unconscious, symbolic plane as well. Horror can be a re-enactment of some long-suppressed fear that has seized a child, even a baby. A dream. A taboo. A fear gets locked in the subconscious... These are contradictory urges – an irresistible attraction and desire for sex and the fear of the unknown and the illicit. The very ambivalence builds tension... Put together correctly the classic horror sequence is the equivalent of the sexual act.[15]*

The relationship between André and the Baron perhaps best illuminates the unconscious struggle at the heart of the film. They are both "of noble heritage", but André, in his French soldier's uniform, represents a new order, which renders the Baron's way of life anachronistic. The old man believes in ghosts and damnation, the young man believes in modern medicine and rationalism. But they both want the same woman – or do they?

Accepting the premise that the Baron evokes André's noble heritage in the form of his father (and this is made plausible by the discussion of André's own father having been guillotined by the revolution for the offense of noble rank) the dream reveals a classic Freudian family romance. Past and present overlap in this dream, in an uneasy way as befits a ghost story, but when the identity of the dreamer's love interest overlaps with that of the father's, the dream becomes a nightmare. Coming face to face with this most incestuous of repressed desires is enough to make anyone wake up screaming.

In his work *On The Nightmare*, Freud's disciple and biographer Ernest Jones extends this idea to account for all nightmares, in a surprising but ultimately intriguing thesis: "an attack of the Nightmare is an expression of a mental conflict over an incestuous desire.[16]" Many new theories have emerged which attempt to modify Freud and Jones's rigid model of wish fulfilment in dreams[17]. Without entering into a discussion of the merits or drawbacks of orthodox Freudian theory, it is safe to assert that, regarding the nightmare as "an expression of mental conflict over an incestuous desire": certainly in **The Terror** it would seem to be so. For it is at the climax of the film (to use Corman's model of "the sexual act") that what has fascinated André (Hélène's ambiguous identity) becomes a source of horror, as Hélène is revealed to be the one woman more taboo to André than any other. In keeping with the paradigm of the family romance, André is only free to fulfil his taboo desire after he has surpassed the Baron and taken his place in relation to the object of their rivalry.

## MONSTERS, PAST AND PRESENT

The conflict between André and the Baron operates on many levels. In this light, Karloff and Nicholson are perfectly suited to their roles: they stand in

complete contrast to one another in appearance, manner and method. Karloff's performance is elegant and mannered, and decidedly "Old World". The brevity of preparation for the part put him at no disadvantage. Trained in a travelling theatre company, he learned to adapt to new roles quickly, once playing 106 different parts in 53 weeks[18].

Nicholson, by contrast, was trained in a version of Method acting, which emphasizes taking time to "become" the role. Often, it would take him up to three weeks into shooting a film to become comfortable with a part, and here the entire shoot lasted only three days[19]. In a hurry to finish shooting, Corman offered little to no direction, and the actors were left to develop their own motivations for their respective characters[20]. One gets the sense that Nicholson is improvising the part, and what results is less acting and more direct gut response. The tension between these methods emphasizes the conflict between the two characters – André is brash, intrusive and glib next to the Baron's restrained and polite gentility. When first informed that he has seen a ghost, André jokes "With all due respect, Baron, for a ghost she's a very active young woman!"

There is a sense that the two men are negotiating an uneasy and symbolic transfer of power, for what has been entirely ignored about this film is the way in which it illuminates a critical moment in horror film history: the passing of the torch from one generation of on-screen monsters to the next. For a brief moment the aging Karloff, the man immortalized as Frankenstein's monster, shares the screen with a very young Nicholson, the man who would become prototypical screen psycho Jack Torrance in **The Shining**. Resignedly, Karloff informs his successor "What you see before you are the remains of a once noble house. Relics. Ghosts of past glory."

Uncannily, this latent transition became manifest five years later, when Peter Bogdanovich edited footage from **The Terror** into his first film, **Targets**. As Bogdanovich tells it:

*What Roger said was "I want you to take twenty minutes of Karloff footage from **The Terror**, then I want you to shoot twenty more minutes with Boris – I've shot whole pictures in two days – and then I want you to shoot another forty minutes with some other actors over ten days. I can take the twenty and the twenty and the forty and I've got a whole new eighty-minute Karloff film. What do you say?*[21]

What Bogdanovich said was "sure", but he made certain to whittle the twenty proposed minutes from **The Terror** down to a mere four minutes at the outset of the film. **Targets** is loosely based on the events surrounding the Texas Tower incident which occurred several years earlier, when ex-Marine Charles Whitman shot and killed sixteen people from a tower on the University of Texas campus. In **Targets**, Bogdanovich cast Karloff as an aging horror film star, whose last film was so dreadful and out of date that it prompted his retirement. The film helped initiate a whole new cycle of horror films and a new kind of true-to-life monster which was to replace the "painted monsters" of Karloff's generation: the modern psycho killer.

In *The Interpretation Of Dreams*[22], Freud posits that interpreting the experience of dreaming is actually a process with several distinct parts: the dream itself, telling the dream (thereby imposing a narrative on an often incoherent set of images) and finally, free-associating to the dream images in order to arrive at an interpretation of the meaning latent in the dream. The relationship between **The Terror** and **Targets** mirrors this process exactly: Corman retroactively imposed a narrative structure on a set of discontinuous images in order for the film to "make sense" to an audience; but it took **Targets** (Bogdanovich's "interpretation") to expose the modern implications of the symbolic transition from Karloff to Nicholson in **The Terror**.

The 1960's ushered in what Charles Derry has referred to as the "horror of personality movie" in his early work on the psychology of horror[23]. Gone were the abstract, symbolic monsters, representing repressed aspects of personality – the monsters of modern horror films were all too often being culled from real-life accounts of calculated mass murder. Made the same year as **Pretty Poison** and **The Boston Strangler**, **Targets** exposes the growing fear and fascination surrounding the myth of the mass murderer in the late 1960's. Up until that point psycho films had generally included a rational psychological explanation for the killer's actions, and had often traced the roots of illness to some childhood trauma.[24] **Targets**, in a dramatic break with tradition, leaves the killer's insanity unexplained, illuminating the truly horrifying idea that monsters are among us everywhere, indistinguishable from the rest of us. "It is the very absence of any reason, the very refusal on Bogdanovich's part to give us the slightest grounds for reassurance, that makes **Targets** so disturbing."[25]

Looking ahead, these elements – latent in **The Terror** and manifest in **Targets** – were to have a profound effect on Nicholson's career. His roles in **The Shining, One Flew Over The Cuckoo's Nest**, and **Batman**, as examples, are all part of a continuum, exploring the unpredictably violent potential of the (inexplicably) "damaged" human mind. In each case, Nicholson conveys the extremes of his character's behaviour, yet leaves room for the viewer to identify with him. This quality is integral to the modern film "psycho", whose behaviour can vacillate between "normal" and over-the-top all in a matter of moments.

As André Duvalier in **The Terror**, Jack Nicholson gives a performance that is not indicative of the actor he would become. None of his trademark effects are evident yet – no lazy, crocodile grin or wildly explosive tantrums. But the movie itself and his role in it foreshadow the direction his career would ultimately take – departing from tradition to lead a new generation of actors into uncharted territory.

# NOTES

1. Corman, Roger (1990) *How I Made A Hundred Movies In Hollywood And Never Lost A Dime*, New York: Random House:94.

2. Silver, Alain and Ursini, James (1994) *More Things Than Are Dreamt Of: Masterpieces Of Supernatural Horror*, New York: Limelight Editions:55.

3. See Weldon, Michael (1983) *The Psychotronic Encyclopedia Of Film*, New York, Ballantine Books.

4. Brode, Douglas (1987) *The Films Of Jack Nicholson*, Toronto, Ontario: Citadel Press: 52.

5. For this and other alternative approaches to previously neglected films see Brottman, Mikita (1997) *Offensive Films: Toward An Anthropology Of Cinema Vomitif*, Westport, Conn: Greenwood Press.

6. Brode (1987):55.

7. **The Fall Of The House Of Usher** (1960), **The Pit And The Pendulum** (1961), **Tales Of Terror** (1962), **The Premature Burial** (1962), **The Raven** (1963), **The Terror** (1963), **The Masque Of The Red Death** (1964), **The Tomb Of Ligeia** (1964). Although Corman went on to make the last two films in the cycle after completing **The Terror**, he had the sense that the Poe work was coming to an end after wrapping **The Raven**. See Corman (1990):88.

8. Corman (1990):89.

9. Bloom, Harold (1999) *Bloom's Major Poets: Edgar Allan Poe*, New York: Chelsea House Publishers:32.

10. **The Old Dark House**, dir. James Whale. Universal Studios, 1932.

11. Freud, Sigmund (1953 [1919]) *The Uncanny*, Standard Edition, vol. XVII: London: Hogarth Press: 225.

12. These archetypal characters and the dynamics between them can also be approached from a Jungian perspective. For more detailed descriptions of the archetypal resonance and mythic qualities of witches, princesses, heroes and others, see both Jung, Carl Gustav (1988) *Dreams*, Princeton: Princeton University Press, and Von Franz, Marie-Louise (1997) *Archetypal Patterns In Fairy Tales*, Toronto, Ontario: Inner City Books.

13. See Freud, Sigmund (1955(1900)) *The Interpretation Of Dreams*, Standard Edition, vols. IV & V, London: Hogarth Press.

14. The film Corman refers to is **The Fall Of The House Of Usher**, made earlier in the Poe cycle.

15. Corman (1990):80.

16. Jones, Ernest (1950) *On The Nightmare*, New York: Grove Press: 44.

17. For a discussion of one of the most recent additions to the field see Hartmann, Ernest (1998) *Dreams And Nightmares: A New Theory On The Origins And Meaning Of Dreams*, New York: Plenum Press.

18. Jensen, Paul M. (1974) *The Films Of Boris Karloff*, Cranbury, NJ: A.S. Barnes and Co: 13.

19. McGilligan, Patrick (1994) *Jack's Life: A Biography Of Jack Nicholson*, New York: W.W.Norton and Co: 133.

20. Jensen (1974):164.

21. Corman (1990):141-2.

22. See Freud, Sigmund (1955 [1900]) *The Interpretation Of Dreams*, Standard Edition, vols IV &V: London: Hogarth Press.

23. See Derry, Charles (1977) *Dark Dreams: A Psychological History Of The Modern Horror Film*, New York: A.S. Barnes and Co.

24. **Psycho** and **Peeping Tom** are examples of this.

25. Derry, Charles (1977):34. This set the tone for many movies to follow, including **Frenzy, 10 Rillington Place, Henry: Portrait Of A Serial Killer**, amongst others. For a chronology of modern psycho films see also McCarty, John (1993) *Movie Psychos And Madmen: Film Psychopaths From Jekyll And Hyde To Hannibal Lector*, New York: Citadel Press.

# 'THE SHOOTING':
# "THE VIRGINIAN ON ACID"

It's easy to forget just how important the Western has been to Jack Nicholson. Besides giving him one of his first tastes of screen acting (in 1962's **The Broken Land**), the genre provided Jack with the subject of his second directing assignment (**Goin' South**) and the chance to work with his hero, Marlon Brando (in Arthur Penn's **The Missouri Breaks**). More importantly still, the American West was the subject of Nicholson's first truly great films, **Ride In The Whirlwind** and **The Shooting**.

## ORIGINS

**The Shooting** was one of four films Jack Nicholson made between the summer of 1965 and the Autumn of 1966. Yes, that's right; Jack Nicholson made *four* feature length movies in one twelve month period. That's compared to the one film every eighteen months that a big star like John Travolta or Nic Cage might make, or the two movies a year that a hardworking character actor like Don Cheadle or Steve Buscemi might appear in. Nicholson's heavy workload was, however, pretty much the standard for anyone employed by Roger Corman, the producer/director whose hectic schedules were second only to his expertise in the field of low budget film-making.

The man behind such quality fare as **The Viking Women And The Sea Serpent** and **Teenage Caveman**, Roger Corman was *the* undisputed king of '60s exploitation cinema. His recipe for success was simple; pack your pictures with tonnes of sex, action, violence and pop culture and cut costs at every corner. Planned as perfunctory exercises in revenue raking, Corman's pictures would achieve a level of retrospective respectability since they also doubled as America's finest unofficial film school. Martin Scorsese, Francis Ford Coppola, Peter Bogdanovich, Joe Dante, James Cameron: they all got their first directing gigs courtesy of the man known as "Corman The Employer". Corman's American International Pictures also handed out work to young writers like Robert Towne (who cooked up a couple of Edgar Allan Poe adaptations before he hitting pay dirt with **The Last Detail** and **Chinatown**), aspiring technicians such as Nic Roeg (who went from lensing **The Masque Of The Red Death** to totally reinventing cinema with **Performance**) and budding actors like Dick Miller, Bruce Dern, William Shatner and Jack Nicholson.

Nicholson's relationship with AIP dated back to 1959 when he became one of a select band of actors who could claim to have starred in their debut feature. That the film in question was the execrable **Cry Baby**

**Killer** effectively explains why Jack's next Corman assignment was a cameo as improbably named masochist Wilbur Force in the director's version of **Little Shop Of Horrors**. After that, Nicholson played a psycho killer in **The Wild Ride**, a misfit cowhand in the aforementioned **The Broken Land** and the marvellously monikered Roxford Bedlo in the Corman-directed **The Raven**. Jack also took the lead in **The Terror**, a horror movie made extraordinary by the fact that it was put together in a couple of days when Corman realised that **The Raven** was going to wrap early.

Jack's duties on the hectic set of **The Terror** also included writing a few vignettes and even directing a couple of scenes. There's actually an old Hollywood rumour that the film was shot in a strange relay with directors such as Nicholson, Scorsese and Francis Coppola taking it in turns at the helm. Another person alleged to have taken part in this bizarre, baton-carrying exercise was Monte Hellman, a theatre director who had created a stir with the first west coast production of Samuel Becket's *Waiting For Godot* and had got his first break for Corman shooting **The Beast From Haunted Cave** (*"Not* completely unlike *Waiting For Godot"* as Hellman told this writer in 1995). Since they had a lot in common (receding hairlines, a passion for European cinema and literature, colourful personal lives, etc.), Hellman and Nicholson soon became friends and production partners. After failing to get a picture about abortion off the ground, the pair went to The Philippines to make **Back Door To Hell** and **Flight To Fury** for producer Robert Lippert. A man who could teach Roger Corman a thing or two about cutting corners, Lippert sent Hellman and Nicholson to Manila by boat, thereby saving on the air fare and money *and* giving the duo time to write the second movie on route. Then, when they arrived, the pair were despatched to the Filipino jungle where they spent several sweaty weeks making the sort of routine programmers they could just have easily made in Los Angeles (Lippert insisted his films be made in The Philippines to keep production costs to a minimum – Corman, never one to miss a trick, shifted his productions to South-East Asia in the 1970s).

On returning to AIP, Jack and Monte, determined to break away from exploitation pictures, went to Roger Corman with the idea of making a Western. Hellman and Nicholson's film wasn't going to be a "some of you stay here and guard the girl, we'll cut them off at the pass" horse opera, however. The picture they envisaged was an existential study, a film with European sensibilities set in the most American of locations. On hearing the pitch, Corman, thought for a moment, then threw up his hands and said; "you can have your movie. But if you're going to make one Western you might as well make two. And make sure there's lots of blood and Indians."

So it was that with Corman's words ringing in their ears and $60,000 of AIP's money in their pockets, Hellman, Nicholson and their tiny crew rode off into the Utah desert. When they returned twelve weeks later, they showed the finished movies to Corman, whose only reaction was to ask where all the Indians were (**The Shooting** features one Native American who revels in the wonderful name of Cuy el Tsosie). Convinced that he couldn't sell the movies in the US, the head of AIP was ready to write the films off a tax loss when Nicholson suggested taking them to the Cannes Film Festival to attract European buyers. When he flew into France with the film cans sitting in his lap, even Jack couldn't seriously have thought that he'd find a distributor. It was a surprise to him as much as anyone else then when critics started to talk about **The Shooting** and **Ride In The Whirlwind** as the underground sensation of Cannes 1965. Shortly afterwards, the films were screened in Paris and their reputation as the most important Westerns of the mid-'60s began to take shape.

## STORY

While the story behind the making of **The Shooting** is eccentric, the tale the film tells is plain absurd. Few critics have been brave enough to analyse Hellman's Western, but even fewer have had the courage to attempt a plot synopsis. One who has is Douglas Brode, author of *The Films Of Jack Nicholson* (1996), a very fine study of Nicholson's screen acting. As this extract from his summary proves, even the doughty Mr Brode can't completely come to terms with **The Shooting**'s complexities:

*It begins and ends with the parallel deaths of two men – or, according to one interpretation, the bizarre double death of the man presumably killed in the opening. A fellow named Coigne is never glimpsed but his presence hangs over the whole story. During the early moments, we learn that Coigne has disappeared. Willet Gashade (Warren Oates) arrives at a mine to discover that his brother, Coigne, is gone. The former bounty hunter attempts to learn from one of his partners why this is so. The semi-retarded Coley (Will Hutchins) tries to explain what happened to their buddy, Leland Drum, who apparently now inhabits a grave near the mine. Coley's rantings are too confusing to allow Willet any understanding of just why Drum is dead, but it is apparent that Coigne was involved in a violent incident in the nearest town, during which a man was ridden down and a child was also killed. But whether Coigne actually did the double murder, or whether the death of Drum is related to any of this, Willet cannot grasp.*

We're only half-an-hour into the movie and you're already probably pretty confused. And from here, **The Shooting** actually becomes even *more* convoluted. A strange woman (Millie Perkins) walks into Willet's camp and tries to buy a horse before offering him even more money to ride with her

across the desert. The nature of the mission nor the eventual destination are never discussed but Willet and Coley join her anyway. On their journey, they are followed by a man on horseback who turns out to be Billy Spear (Jack Nicholson), a bounty killer who may or may not have had something to do with the death of Drum – that's if Drum is dead, of course. When the woman's horse dies, Spear insists Coley give his mount to her, only to then leave the idiot savant at the mercy of the desert. But instead of dying, Coley stumbles upon a dead man's horse and rejoins the group, only to then be shot by Spear. Incensed, Willet wrestles the gunslinger to the ground and breaks his hand. It's then that he wheels around to find that the woman has vanished – if, that is, she ever existed in the first place.

Willet later arrives in a canyon where he finds the woman involved in a gunfight. He tries to intervene as he seems to recognise her victim but it's too late. Shots are fired and both the woman and her rival (whose face we never see) fall to the floor. Willet is also injured in the melee, but as he dies (if, indeed, he is dying) he summons up all his power to utter one last word (if, indeed, etc.); "Coigne!" As Brode concludes his synopsis: "Is Willet joining his brother, who he now realises is dead, as he too soon will be? Or is he going to survive, but realises that his brother is the man the woman has been following, suggesting that she may have been the wife and mother of the man and child killed back in town?". Indeed.

## ANALYSIS

Deliberately obtuse, purposefully absurd, **The Shooting** would be bloody annoying were not so much of it so good. Rather like other obscurist classics such as Orson Welles' **Touch Of Evil** and Nic Roeg's **The Man Who Fell To Earth**, Hellman's film is so intriguing and entertaining that you really don't care that you can't always tell what's going on. The director's work alone elevates the film above the other American-made Westerns of its age, with Hellman transforming Utah's Zion Park into a truly alien landscape. Carole Eastman's screenplay, meanwhile, bestows a complexity upon stock Western characters like the hired hand and bounty killer that gives them with more in common with the cinema of Antonioni than the films of John Ford (it's not unknown for art house cinemas to screen **The Shooting** and **Ride In The Whirlwind** together with Jack's Antonioni picture **The Passenger**). Eastman's script also makes thematic references to the novels of Jack London and the works of Albert Camus. The allusions to the latter are particularly interesting given that, at the time the film was being assembled, director, producer and writer were all reading the existentialist's essay on the myth of Sisyphus (the figure from Greek mythology damned to spend eternity pushing a rock up a hill only to watch it roll back down upon reaching the summit). Nicholson even acknowledged Camus' influence in interviews, stating that; "man's only dignity in life is in his return down the mountain after pushing the stone up. That's what our film's about." That this European thinking is mixed together with all sorts of familiar Western staples lead a critic at the time to describe **The Shooting** as "not unlike watching an episode of *The Virginian* on acid"; lazy journalism, sure, but if you've seen the film, you know what he's getting at.

Hellman and Eastman's exemplary work is complemented by a clutch of fine performances. Quite simply the finest character actor of his generation, Warren Oates is on superbly sweaty form as Willet Gashade. Also excellent in Hellman's **Two-Lane Blacktop**, **Cockfighter** and **China 9, Liberty 37**, Oates imbues Gashade not only with a range contradictions but with a quality that suggests he is forever thinking – an amazing feat given that Willet is essentially a pretty dumb character. He is brilliantly supported by Millie Perkins as the enigmatic woman, and by Will Hutchins as Coley.

If Oates is the very best thing about **The Shooting** (as he was the best thing about virtually all of the films he appeared in), the picture's most eye-catching performance comes from Jack Nicholson. Just 29 at the time the film was made, the first thing you notice about Jack is that, well... he looks *really* young. Slim at the waist and with most of his own hair still intact, he's a far cry from the portly, balding Nicholson we've all grown to love (as in **The Border**, a later film in which Jack again co-stars with Warren Oates). More intriguing than Nicholson's appearance, though, is his performance, about which the main points of interest are that i) Billy Spear is one of the few out-and-out bad guys Jack has played and ii) the leather-clad cowboy looks kind of homosexual.

Although a lot of his characters have had dark halves, Nicholson has played few real villains during his forty-year career and of those he has played, most have been of the cartoon/pantomime variety (The Joker, Darryl Van Horne and Colonel Nathan R. Jessop all belong to the "he's behind you" school of screen villainy). Sneering, super creep Billy Spear stands apart from Jack's other bad guy turns on the grounds that he possesses a genuine sense of evil. Since the script gives him little to say and even less time in which to say it, it's entirely up to Nicholson to generate an aura of malevolence. He does so, in part, through his brilliant use of body-language; Spear's hands-on-hips stance and crooked lips create all sorts of ugly, unembracable angles to subtly spell out his villainy. For the main source of the gunslinger's menace, you need to examine the strange weariness Nicholson brings to the role. Rather like Jonathan in the latter stages of **Carnal Knowledge**, Spear has a peculiar lethargy about him. As is appropriate to a film made under the aegis of the Poe-obsessed Roger Corman, he strikes us a man who is used up; an old soul who is approaching the end of the trail. It is this sensation of being in close proximity to death then that might explain why Spear makes for such an effective bad guy. Quite how a 29-year-old actor was able to produce such sombre sleepiness is hard to say. It could be that Nicholson was tapping into his personal misfortune; at the time **The Shooting** was made, Jack was experiencing difficulties in his marriage and had severe anxieties about how his career. Then again, it might have just as much to do with the fact that Jack Nicholson is a mighty fine actor.

If you are to fully appreciate the darkness of Billy Spear, you need to compare it with the gentle, boyishness of Wes, the cow-hand character Nicholson wrote for himself in **The Shooting**'s sister film, **Ride In The Whirlwind**. Another tale of mysterious motives and destinationless journeys, **Ride...** allowed Jack to show off the sunnier aspects of his personality. It's only when the two films are seen together that you can really enjoy the Jekyll and Hyde effect that Jack was clearly going for. Of course, Wes's easy, rolling charm would remain a feature of Nicholson's work throughout the '70s. Spear's cobra eyes and insincere smile, on the other hand, would be something Jack would leave well alone until he worked with Stanley Kubrick on **The Shining**, fourteen years later.

When he discussed Nicholson's performance in **The Shooting** in 1995, Monte Hellman was careful to point out that, for him, Jack's work was not the most significant aspect of the picture. "As far as I'm concerned, **The Shooting** was Warren Oates' movie. I'd seen some of Warren's earlier pictures and TV work and decided that I wanted to work with him. And when I did work with him, I decided I never really wanted to work with anyone else. He was an amazing talent. Of course, Jack's also a pretty amazing actor. I think what's most remarkable about Billy Spear is just how appalling the character is – a really horrible human being. That's what surprised people. It certainly surprised people on the set, because away from filming, Jack's so funny and witty and charming. Do I think his personal life informed the part? That's not for me to say. I know that his wife has said that there is something within Jack that's broken and can't ever be fixed and it's true that he had a very tough childhood. But I prefer to think it's all down to Jack being such a great actor. He was pretty good as the Devil in **Witches Of Eastwick** and no-one ever suggested he was Satan. So I think it's safe to assume that he could play a gun-killer without having had something dreadful happen to him personally."

One of the few things rarer than Nicholson playing nasty is the sight of Jack playing homosexual. So straight that he makes Arnold Schwarzenegger look effeminate, it's almost impossible to conceive of Nicholson playing a man who isn't attracted to women. But, in truth, there isn't an awful lot to suggest that Billy Spear is queer, either. That said, Jack's dandefied costume isn't the most masculine ever seen in a Western. Spanish-style Stetson, black gloves, white shirt and tightly-worn leather waistcoat.

Unlike **Carnal Knowledge** however, which can easily be read as a gay man's struggle to come to terms with his sexuality, there's little else in **The Shooting** to mark Spear out as homosexual. Even Jack's rather unfortunate costume provides evidence of his acting talent rather than of his character's orientation. Dressed in his close-fitting duds, you appreciate that Jack Nicholson isn't a particularly big man. He isn't like Clint Eastwood who can use his 6' 4" frame to impose authority upon any situation. No, Nicholson, at least before he piled on the pounds, has to produce power from within. In **The Shooting**, a spindly Jack generates the sort of energy much larger actors would struggle to summon up. As Monte Hellman puts it; "He's like a laser. He can focus his energy so tightly it makes him look like a giant, when in fact he's just a balding guy with a weight problem." This "laser beam" quality certainly played a part in making Billy Spear one of the more memorable screen bad guys of the Hollywood West.

Spear is so memorable, in fact, that you wonder why Nicholson hasn't dedicated more of his time towards exploring his nasty side. One possible explanation is that he simply hasn't been offered the roles. Another might be that, until very recently, it was difficult to make a living and nigh on impossible to achieve stardom by playing crooks and psychos. While Gary Oldman and John Malkovich have done very well out of villainy, a quick look at those of Jack's contemporaries who allowed themselves to be typecast as heavies, like Bruce Dern, proves that back then it was a hell of a lot easier to make bucks beating up bad guys.

**The Shooting** certainly didn't do much to improve Jack's standing in Hollywood. As the aforementioned Eastwood leapfrogged to fame on the back of Sergio Leone's **Dollars** movies, Nicholson would spend three more years writing screenplays (**The Trip** and The Monkees' vehicle **Head**) and starring in biker movies (**Rebel Rousers, Hell's Angels On Wheels**) before he finally hit the road to the big time.

It would take even longer for **The Shooting** and **Ride In The Whirlwind** to be recognised as important cinematic works. Immediately embraced in France, the pictures were dismissed out of hand by American critics as typical Corman co-productions. And it wasn't until the '70s and the release of revisionist Westerns like **Solider Blue, Ulzana's Raid** and **Little Big Man** that people rediscovered Hellman's work and concluded that the genre had actually started to mutate as early as the mid-'60s. So great did interest in the two pictures become that one ambitious student penned a study in which the shaky, documentary-style camerawork used in the final shoot-out sequence was compared with the famous Zapruda footage of the Kennedy assassination. The finished dissertation was lauded by critics the world over.

## CODA

Now appreciated as the important, mythic works Nicholson and Hellman had always figured them to be, **The Shooting** and **Ride In The Whirlwind** function on so many levels that they actually stand up pretty well to academic analysis. If this article seems a little light on such *Sight & Sound*-style discussion, it's because it would be foolish to start analysing a film that, owing to its limited availability on video, most of you probably aren't that familiar with. So now you know something about both the picture and Nicholson's fine supporting turn, do everything in your power to track down **The Shooting** and deconstruct it to your heart's content. But, and this is the other reason for not attempting too detailed a study of the movie here, be warned: you don't need to dig very far to find out just how queer a fish **The Shooting** is. Indeed, this is one oddball movie that is quite happy to fess up to its own ambiguity. As Oates' Willet Gashade remarks at one point; "I don't see no point to it". "There isn't any," Millie Perkins' mystery lady replies.

# "ALIENATING ALIENATION": DECONSTRUCTING THE ANTI-HERO IN 'FIVE EASY PIECES'

*The actor is Camus's ideal existential hero, because if life is absurd, and the idea is to live a more vital life, therefore the man who lives more lives is in a better position than the guy who lives just one.*
—Jack Nicholson[1]

Following his film-stealing performance as George Hanson, the pot-smoking, alcoholic lawyer in Dennis Hopper's **Easy Rider** (1969), Jack Nicholson sought to consolidate and expand his newly minted screen persona as the "Counterculture Movie Star",[2] or, more colourfully, "The Mad American Rebel".[3] Already touted as an actor of extraordinary range and intelligence who embodied the anti-establishment disillusionment of the 1960s Vietnam War generation, Nicholson began looking strategically at scripts that involved deeply flawed yet recognizably human characters in complex psychological and social situations. These are what Nicholson himself has called "cusp characters", alienated loners that question traditional middle class values by straddling the narrow margin between self-delusion and disillusion, while refusing to fit conveniently into preconceived societal or narrative moulds.[4] "You've got to keep attacking the audience and their values," avowed Nicholson. "If you pander to them, you lose your vitality."[5]

The actor found exactly the screen vehicle he was looking for in the character of Robert Dupea, the charismatic yet morally vacuous protagonist of Bob Rafelson's **Five Easy Pieces** (1970), a troubled, doppelganger-type role with which Nicholson later admitted a close philosophical empathy.[6] A critical and popular success, **Five Easy Pieces** turned out to be a seminal film. This was true both for the actor – it laid the foundation for every self-reflexive, theatrically gestic Nicholson performance in the decade that followed (climaxing with the role of David Locke in Michelangelo Antonioni's **The Passenger** [1975]) – and the national psyche as a whole. Released in September 1970, two years after the violent repression of the student left following the events of May 1968 in Paris and the yippee debacle at the Chicago Democratic National Convention later that same year, Rafelson's film defined a profound moral soul-searching and growing ambivalence towards counter-cultural politics in general. In this sense it exemplified a trend that had become increasingly prevalent in a number of films during the Nixon era (not least Nicholson's own 1971 directorial debut, **Drive, He Said**, which was extremely critical of '60s youth culture). Significantly the release of **Five Easy Pieces** came just four months after the tragic events at Kent State in 1970, when National Guardsmen shot and killed four protesting students on the Ohio campus. That same week, Nixon escalated the war in Vietnam by sending ground troops into Cambodia.

In the face of this conservative backlash, the left seemed disillusioned and in disarray, fractured by ideological infighting and a growing feeling of political impotence. Film scholar Robert B. Ray has noted that this shift in the political zeitgeist – scepticism toward both the left and the right – opened the doors for a new kind of Hollywood persona:

*The period's self-consciousness about the received American myths... promoted a new kind of star, who in Classic Hollywood might have operated only in the margins of straight genre movies... essentially character actors whose self-reflexive, self-doubting personae contrasted sharply with the confident, natural imperturbability of Cooper, Grant, Gable, and Wayne. While the classic stars had depended on the cumulative power of typecasting and genre conventions, these new performers specialized in playing against the expectations created either by a film's nominal genre or by their own previous roles.*[7]

Their model was, of course, Marlon Brando who, as a 1950s Oedipal anti-hero, affected a mannered, often theatrically campy style to distance himself from studio formulae. Nicholson will take this self-reflexivity a significant step further, eschewing a stable screen identity (or more accurately, anti-identity in the form of an indefinable anti-hero) in favour of acting out different personae as a means of exploring and exploding the interpellating roles of phallic masculinity, patriarchy and their corollary, bourgeois individuality.

Nicholson's strong identification with Bobby Dupea is hardly surprising given that **Five Easy Pieces** was written with Nicholson specifically in mind by his old acting school crony Carole Eastman (writing as "Adrien Joyce"). The character of Bobby is based on her close personal friendship with the actor.[8] Filmed on a "bargain basement" budget of $800,000, the film was released by BBS Productions (Rafelson, in collaboration with Bert Schneider) through Columbia Pictures. It was to be the first of Nicholson's five acting collaborations with the director.[9] A relative newcomer to film at that time, Rafelson had made his mark in television as the creative force (with Schneider) behind The Monkees' NBC television series. He subsequently directed the ersatz mop tops' first and only feature film, **Head** (1968), which was co-produced and co-scripted by Nicholson.

Rafelson was a natural choice to direct **Five Easy Pieces**, for his early films explore the slippery nature of personal identity, specifically the possibilities of self-discovery and persona construction when characters of differing temperaments and social backgrounds are forced into a common crisis or milieu. Eschewing linear plot for character study, Rafelson's narratives are elusive and elliptical, often revolving around what Jay Boyer has called "a partnering of opposites."[10] As one might expect, his characters are explored less in terms of the Oedipal psychological profiles typified by the Hollywood mainstream or *film noir* than by dissonant, incomplete narratives where complex, contradictory, usually protean characters are thrust into contexts that exacerbate rather than synthesize the antinomies in character dialectic.[11] They thus have far more in common with the films of European *auteurs* such as Alain Resnais, Marguerite Duras and Antonioni than other Nicholson directors of that time such as Vincente Minnelli or Mike Nichols.

"If my films have anything in common," says Rafelson, "it's that they tend to focus on characters who are struggling to overcome the burden of tradition in their lives."[12] His protagonists tend to be defined reactively by pressures from without, specifically their resistance to the interpellated role that they are forced to occupy as an already-formed subject, rather than from their own ego-driven agency.[13] Consequently, the journey or "process of becoming" in Rafelson's films is often more important than the destination, which helps to explain his interest in more marginal, counter-cultural figures – idealists and wanderers, caught between dream and reality – rather than pragmatic action-heroes. As Boyer has noted, Rafelson thus deconstructs the myths that nurture the idea of the American Dream – the necessity of agency, mobility and the teleological search for an ultimate goal – thereby foreclosing the elements essential for the traditional Hollywood protagonist setting out to conquer the uncertain road ahead. Instead, this road often leads to impasse or nothingness, while the search more closely resembles an impossible flight. The resulting existential aporia reflects the protagonist's often futile response to the imposition of identity or class conditions from without, and his fatal inability to generate individual agency.

This reactive tendency – what Nietzsche famously called "ressentiment" – accurately describes Nicholson's Bobby Dupea, who has a much greater sense of who he is not, rather than who he is or might become. To all outward appearances, Bobby is a working class, good ol' boy who short times as a hard-hat roustabout in a Southern Californian oil field with his redneck friend Elton (Billy "Greene" Bush). His clinging, kewpie doll girlfriend is Rayette Dipesto (Karen Black), who works as a waitress at a local diner but aspires to a singing career in the mould of her country music idol, Tammy Wynette. Through a series of short-but-telling vignettes, Rafelson paints the hard-living Bobby's character and lifestyle as a series of poker and

bowling games, extended drinking bouts and promiscuous one-night stands, punctuated by a series of cantankerous arguments with Rayette and Elton over music, love and marriage.

Exasperated with Rayette (who's pregnant with his child and is threatening suicide if he leaves her), Bobby drives south to Los Angeles to visit his neurotic, insecure sister, Partita (Lois Smith), a classically trained pianist who's in the middle of a frustratingly difficult recording session. Delighted to see him, she informs Bobby that his father has recently suffered two strokes and may never recover: "Don't you think it's right that you should see him, at least once?" she asks him. Bobby, who hasn't visited the family's island home on Puget Sound in over three years, reluctantly agrees to take Rayette on the long drive north to Washington State. Along the way, they pick up Palm Apodaca (Helena Kallianiotes) and Terry Grouse (Toni Basil), whose car has overturned while en route to Alaska. The aggressive, obnoxious Palm is obsessed with dirt and filth, expressing her innate hostility toward the world via an endless tirade of dire ecological foreboding. They're headed to Alaska because it's very clean: "I saw a picture of it... It appeared to look very white to me" (i.e. it's a travel brochure concept of Alaska, a simulacrum). Bobby quickly senses what a pipedream it is: "Yup", he says, "That was before the big thaw." During a stop at a roadside diner, Bobby's unsuccessful attempts to order a side of toast (the film's notorious "Chicken Salad Sandwich" scene) end with him humiliating the waitress and violently clearing their drinks from the table. Increasingly irritated at Palm's incessant negativity, Bobby finally ejects the two hitchhikers and leaves Rayette at a motel with a promise to call her after he's checked out the family situation.

It turns out that far from being the working class roughneck we observed in the film's opening half hour, Bobby is in fact a talented pianist in his own right, raised in a cultured, intellectual upper-middle-class family. Unfortunately, this prodigal son's home life is currently even more alienating and dysfunctional than when Bobby left it three years earlier. Nicholas Dupea (William Challee), the wealthy family patriarch, is unable to speak and confined to a wheelchair. He's attended by a male nurse named Spicer (John Ryan), for whom the repressed Pertita has a less-than-concealed sexual attraction. Meanwhile, much to Bobby's vindictive amusement, his pretentious, fiddle-playing brother, Carl (Ralph Waite) is forced to wear a neck brace following a serious bicycle accident. Carl is engaged to marry the self-confidently beautiful Catherine Van Oost (Susan Anspach), a talented concert pianist who is also his student.

Bobby is immediately attracted to Catherine, who cannot understand why he relinquished a promising career in music for the seemingly inconsequential and unrewarding life of a drifter. Following some initial sparring, the pair sleep together, although it's unclear whether Bobby is genuinely interested in pursuing the romance or is simply using Catherine to get back at his brother's pompous superiority. In any case, their budding relationship is quickly nipped by the unexpected arrival of Rayette, who's left the motel after running out of money. Rafelson's trademark "partnering of opposites" reaches full fruition as some obvious class differences rear their ugly head for the final time. Bobby is doubly embarrassed by Rayette's coarseness and lack of intellectual refinement as well as Carl's obvious glee in leading her on in front of the whole family.

Caught between the jaws of Carl's bourgeois pretension and Rayette's working class lack of sophistication, Bobby makes a final, desperate play for Catherine, who tells him that he's incapable of feeling true emotion, even less equipped to pursue a committed relationship: "When a person who has no love for himself," she tells him, "no respect for himself, no love of his friends, family, work... something... How could he ask for love in return? I mean, why should he ask for it?" Rejected and embarrassed, Bobby tries to justify his life's choices to his stone-faced father in a touching early morning scene on a bluff by the Sound. His eyes welling with tears, he justifies his decisions and rationalizes giving up his musical career in a plaintive one-way conversation. The film ends as Bobby leaves the Dupea home for the last time accompanied

by Rayette. After stopping at a gas station, Bobby abandons his girlfriend, the car, and all his belongings and hitches a ride on an Alaska-bound logging truck. Once again, another new persona is fashioned from a reactive line of flight.

As Robert Ray has noted, **Five Easy Pieces** is typical of many leftist films of the Nixon era, identifying contemporary malaise and its possible solutions as a series of baffling problems with no easy answers. This contrasts with contemporary conservative films of the political Right – **Dirty Harry**, **The French Connection**, **Death Wish** – which artificially highlight and then proselytize the need for a strong individual hero to stand up to the bad guys in the light of ineffectual fence-sitting on the part of the liberal-humanist legal system. On the other hand, despite its elliptical, disjointed narrative style, **Five Easy Pieces** is structured quite conventionally, favouring an exaggerated dialectical opposition between its competing social forces, all the better to illustrate and advocate the obvious need for either *rapprochement* or deconstruction. Thus the vast artificial divide between the intellectual upper class and the more somatic and sensual lower class is expressed through the dialectic between Bobby's musical family, with their predilection for the weighty, ponderous romanticism of Chopin and Brahms, and the oversexed Rayette's sentimental, melodramatic penchant for Tammy Wynette's heart-on-her-sleeve *Stand By Your Man* and *D.I.V.O.R.C.E.* This division is further polarized geographically by the stark contrast in landscape – stunningly shot by Laszlo Kovacs – between the Pacific Northwest and Central California. The Dupea family's stunted, repressed emotions are expressed through the cold, misty remoteness of island life on Washington's Puget Sound as well as the hermetic, almost inbred nature of their various physical and psychological afflictions. Bobby's spiritual and moral barrenness is evoked through the hot, dusty, California oil fields, an arid landscape pockmarked by nodding donkeys and the tangled steel skeletons of ubiquitous oil derricks, a frontier environment where representations of home and family life are satirized through the parodic clichés of Okie trailer trash.

Obviously, this is less an accurate description of the complex, changeable nature of real life in 1970s America than an attempt to paint a timeless, archetypal conflict between seemingly irreconcilable cultures and subjectivities. With the exception of Palm's ecological rant against rampant commercial development, there's no mention of Vietnam, the Civil Rights movement, student protest or the period's burgeoning feminism. This relative lack of dynamic in the traditional dialectic is crucial to understanding and explicating Bobby's political and emotional nihilism, because a more topical discursive framework would have counterpointed Bobby's solipsism with the alternative of collective action and a broader class movement that might supersede his egocentric individualism. This would, in short, create a more overtly Marxist filmic discourse, which the film opts to express only obliquely.

On the other hand, this exaggerated social dialectic is also the source of the film's performative radicalism, disclosing its hidden Brechtian, Epic dimension. Indeed the key to appreciating the complexities and nuances of Nicholson's performance lies in the very doppelganger structure of the narrative itself. For the first thirty minutes, we're drawn into Bobby's persona as a working class rogue. Nicholson pulls out all the stops, accentuating an inarticulate Southern drawl (we seem to be in Texas or the deep South rather than the relative sophistication of the West Coast), and recycling his George Hanson mannerisms from **Easy Rider**: the expansive body language with the flapping arms, darting arched eyebrows and that trademark killer smile, what Alexander Walker once described as a "dazzling, yard-wide smile which can give Nicholson instant sunniness or sexual menace which makes him both attractive-looking and dangerous."[14]

Many critics at the time praised Nicholson for the naturalism of his acting, to the point that the actor seemed to be playing himself. However, as the film progresses, certain cracks start to appear in this realistic facade, and we realize that this apparent naturalism is actually a contrived persona – one among many. Beneath the benign surface of the good 'ol boy there lurks an impulsive violence that Bobby's impassive, placid exterior and measured vocal

accents are trying to repress. Occasionally the facade slips, leading to occasional explosions, such as the fit of rage in his car as he tries to leave Rayette, the rambunctious sex with Betty, and the end of the Chicken Salad Sandwich scene when he sweeps the water glasses from the table. More importantly, this impulsive side is inextricably linked to Bobby's repression of his class background. In the diner, for example, his violent rebellion is completely lacking a true moral centre because he aims it at the unfortunate waitress, not the management, thereby conflating the working class with the rules of the establishment that a more acutely Marxist analysis would naturally hold in opposition. Indeed, the Los Angeles novelist Steve Erickson has gone so far as to associate Bobby's lack of true political consciousness with that of the actor himself, arguing that "Nicholson's rebellion hasn't been against the System, or against those who push its buttons. It's been against the System's flunkies... It's been a demonstration of contempt by the Hip for those too ugly or frightened or already beaten down by the System not to be unhip."[15]

This sense of displaced snobbery concealed behind the mask of the regular Joe is also present in an early scene when, during a lunch break with Elton, Bobby learns that Rayette is pregnant with his child. A father himself, Elton encourages him to accept the responsibility of parenthood, to marry

Rayette and settle down. Heaven knows, claims Elton, he might even get to like it (underlining the film's ongoing dialectic of responsibility vs. imprisonment). Bobby spits contemptuously: "It's ridiculous. I'm sittin' here listening to some cracker asshole who lives in a trailer park comparing his life to mine. Keep on tellin' me about the good life, Elton, because it makes me puke." For the first time, we become aware that perhaps Bobby is not actually working class, for this dialogue indicates an alienated disillusion with the role of the proletariat and middle American values that reflects his thinly veiled elitism. Bobby clearly has no faith in the collective power of the working class to lead any sort of revolution, cultural or otherwise.

Our suspicions are confirmed when Bobby visits his sister Tita at the recording studio. The Southern drawl is quickly abandoned in favour of Nicholson's deliberate, nasal New Jersey twang; his body seems to shrink in gestic understatement; while his obvious knowledge of the keyboard suggests untapped reserves of artistic talent. Everything that has gone before is suddenly re-constructed retroactively as a performance, a masquerade. Nicholson's apparently transparent naturalism appears startlingly contrived and opaque – yet another mask to try on and then discard.

We see evidence of this performative self-reflexivity in a telling scene at the bowling alley, where Bobby openly flirts with two women – Betty (Sally Struthers) and Twinky (Marlena MacGuire). Twinky is convinced that she's seen Bobby on television selling cars. Bobby rises to the bait and flashes his seductive grin: he's good at it, clearly well rehearsed at picking up promiscuous strangers. Betty thinks he's wearing a wig, because on the TV he's mostly bald. Bobby: "Yeah, your friend's real sharp. I don't wear the wig on TV because if you're gonna be out there in front of two and a half million people you've got to be sincere. I mean, I like to wear it when I'm in bowlin' alleys and slippin' around and stuff like that. I think it gives me a little class. What d'you think?" We immediately become aware of a series of multiple masquerades, where the outward mask hides still more masks. In this case, the outward mask is that of a working class man aspiring to be and appear as something better, something that (we subsequently learn) the classical musician Robert Dupea already is. Bobby both negates and reinforces his own class status by acting out a deferred desire for an identity that he already possesses (and yet despises). As film critic Beverly Walker perceptively reminds us, "Nicholson's brilliance is his obvious, intelligent gift for both embodying and commenting upon his character in one seamless evocation. He forgives them their trespasses even as he renders them utterly transparent."[16]

In his provocative and insightful study of the de-construction of masculinity in the films of Nicholson, James Stewart and Clint Eastwood, Dennis Bingham takes Walker's observation a significant step further, noting that Nicholson's overt self-consciousness turns many of his films into a form of absurdist theatre, creating enough distanciation from the revisionist role of the counter-cultural protagonist that his characters become a means of deconstructing alternative narrative forms and genres as such. This opens up a critical space for audience critique, insofar as we become aware of the constructed nature of all social and cultural personae. In **Five Easy Pieces**, in addition to revising the 1950s "rebel male" persona of a Brando or a James Dean, this absurdism is directed back at Nicholson himself, so that the masculine identity of the 1960s anti-hero is also called into question through a form of defamiliarizing masquerade:

*Unlike the rebel males, whose rebellion was often against such bogeys as femininity and "momism" ...he excelled in roles that posed the male as not so much a player of the game as a player of parts, with the codes of masculinity reduced to a series of roles, sensitivity just another in the repertoire... He made a masquerade of masculine conformity, revealing a character's confident male identity as an unconscious oedipal identification with monstrous paternity.*[17]

Masquerade foregrounds gender and social roles as performed constructions rather than manifestations of essence or nature. In this sense, it takes the form of what Brecht calls a social gest, defamiliarizing corporeal signs – e.g. heroic heterosexual virility – as fractured discontinuities, all the better to critique them as multiple ideological fabrications. Psychologically, the term derives from Joan Riviere's seminal 1929 essay, "Womanliness As Masquerade". Here, Riviere claims that women who aspire to the cultural power that masculinity makes possible put on a contrived mask of womanliness and femininity in order to avert anxiety and retribution from patriarchal society as punishment for the woman's castrating threat to its prevailing phallocentrism. The woman thus acts out an overt femininity (playing the role that men want her to play as "the submissive female") as a mask or front behind which she can conceal her true subversive intentions. However, because the enacted femininity and "true" femininity are both patriarchal constructions, they ultimately amount to the same thing.[18] According to Bingham, Nicholson switches the gender roles by employing masquerade in order to play the role of being a "Man" (or, in the context of the early 1970s, its counter-cultural corollary, the alienated "rebel"), just as he plays the role of being a "Star". At the same time however, he presents it as a pose, a role synonymous with male identity and star power as such. The mask is thus performed opaquely as a mask, with the "real" self displaced as yet one more mirror image in a series of commodified simulacra. As Bingham explains it, "Nicholson brings to his simulation a sense of the individual that is itself simulated. This creates an awareness of the character

as a construction separate from the actor – who himself might be a simulation – and from concepts of unified male subjectivity."[19] This allows the actor to walk the tightrope between normality and difference within the split subjectivity of the same character (to the point that they become indistinguishable), leaving us with an unanswerable question: what actually lies behind the mask, other than more simulacra?

This is not an unfamiliar acting strategy. It resembles a postmodern variation on Brecht's Epic Theatre of the 1930s, a theory of performance based on distanciation or *Verfremdungseffekt*, in which the actor observes himself in the act of performing, all the better to estrange the audience from direct psychological (and by extension, social) identification, thereby encouraging critique.[20] Nicholson, by contrast, tends to sacrifice Brecht's interest in the ideological ramifications of social gest in favour of a performative construction – a masquerade mask – that is pleasurable in and for itself. Performance thus overrides competence; the affective takes precedence over the active, creating what Nicholson himself calls an "affectation of style".[21] By turning "masculinity" into a performance, a ritual mask, Nicholson transforms Bobby Dupea into a representation of alienated "Man", forcing a unitary masculinity to break down, in Brechtian fashion, into a "series of comportments" or gests.[22] Instead of identifying with the character, Nicholson observes, reads and narrates him – i.e. mediates him – in the very act of performing him, thus opening up an analytical space for the audience to view the character/actor as a social and narrative construction, both *en acte* and "an act".

The star quality of Nicholson-as-actor merely serves to reinforce this *Verfremdungseffekt*, because his characters are both narrative constructions and star constructions at the same time, mediations of mediations.[23] This sets up a dialectic between involvement and distanciation that mirrors Bobby's own ambivalence within the narrative itself. This is clearly manifested in the scene in the gas station restroom prior to his abandoning Rayette and hitching a ride to Alaska. He removes his jacket, wipes his lips, coughs, takes a piss. A moment of decision. He looks in the bathroom mirror, his hands on each side of the glass so that he's leaning in at his own reflection. He stares at his double: his past, present and future coming into an alignment of becoming. But it's also possible that he's looking to see if there's anything there at all, anything other than yet another mask, another simulacrum. This uncertainty creates an instability that is both unnerving – both Bobby and the audience seem to have lost track of an authentic masculine identity – and pleasurable: this is the sheer compulsion of Nicholson's theatrical skill.

The efficacy of this strategy in **Five Easy Pieces** is reinforced by the fact that Bobby's Oedipal relationship to patriarchy – his rejection of his anointed role within the Symbolic Order – is inextricably intertwined with his potential line of flight: his musical art. As a musical prodigy turned prodigal son, Bobby is an anti-hero insofar as he's refused to follow the hero-musician path mapped out for him (exemplified by his middle name, Eroica, with its suggestion of Beethoven's genius and Napoleon's heroic individualism). In Lacanian terms, lack of identity is rooted in lack of patriarchal recognition and reconciliation. There's no alternative to the rule of the Symbolic Order except through the Imaginary (represented here by music), yet Bobby has refused this because it is associated with, and directed by, the Name of the Father.

We see the import of this impasse in the scene just prior to Bobby's seduction of Catherine, where she asks him to play for her. He studiously picks out the opening phrases from Chopin's *Prelude In E Minor*. This is one of the "Five Easy Pieces" of the film's title that Bobby played as a child to help him practice classical fingering positions. As he performs, the camera pans left across the room, past a rapt and intent Catherine, and focuses on a series of framed photographs of famous composers and the Dupea children as youthful prodigies – Tita, Carl and Bobby. Significantly, the group also includes Nicholas Dupea, looking like a demented Victorian patriarch, his eyes flashing with madness. In this simple shot, Rafelson conflates Bobby's family and his rejection of the Name of the Father with the equally daunting patriarchy of the musical heritage that he's abandoned: a double rebellion against both the Symbolic and the Imaginary.

If, as we've seen, Nicholson's performance amounts to a series of assumed identities, what then are we to make of the film's emotive climax, when Bobby confronts his paralyzed father on the bluff next to the Sound? The scene is usually described as an acting tour-de-force, with Nicholson not only discovering hitherto untapped emotional reserves, but also tailoring the scene to his own individual persona by writing his own dialogue.

The scene opens in long shot silhouette, as Bobby wheels his father alongside the Sound at dusk and tries to find some measure of communication and understanding before he leaves, probably for the last time. It's necessarily a one-way conversation, as Bobby kneels down in front of his father's wheelchair like a supplicant and tries to explain himself:

"I don't know if you'd be particularly interested in hearing anything about me – my life – most of it doesn't add up to much that I could relate as a way of life that you'd approve of. I move around a lot. Not because I'm looking for anything, really, but because I'm getting away from things that get bad if I stay. Auspicious beginnings, you know what I mean?"

The rest is uttered tearfully as Bobby tries not to break down. He sighs, looks away, rarely looking at his father as he speaks:

"I'm trying to imagine your half of this conversation. My feeling is, I don't know, that if you could talk we wouldn't be talking. It's pretty much the way that it got to be before I left... I don't know what to say. (He cries briefly). Tita suggested that we try to... I don't know... I think that she feels that we've got some understanding to reach. But she totally denies the fact that we were never that comfortable with one another to begin with. The best that I can do is apologize. We both know that I was never really that good at it anyway. I'm sorry it didn't work out."

There was a great deal of disagreement between Nicholson, Rafelson and Eastman on how to perform this scene. Rafelson wanted Bobby to reach deep inside himself and to sob to the extent that he could no longer continue with his speech. Nicholson felt that this was out of character, rejecting any suggestion of self-pity in Bobby. Rafelson didn't see the scene that way: "I maintained that Dupea was crying because of agony over the life he was leading, and that this agony had to be revealed", he said. "Finally, I said, 'Jack, this is bullshit, you don't want to do it because you can't.'"[24]

Nicholson, who'd co-scripted Rafelson's **Head** and had an excellent feel for writing a key scene that would give his role a little baroque flourish, delayed writing the scene until the day of the shoot. Suddenly, he found the hidden dynamic that he felt was the driving force of the film, coming up with the phrase "auspicious beginnings" to describe Bobby's youthful promise as a musician and to trigger the necessary emotion. "The fact that I was playing it as an allegory of my own career is the secret there," admitted Nicholson: "Auspicious beginnings."[25] The actor admitted in an interview at the time that he was in conflict with Rafelson over the scene "because he fears my lacking 'sentimentality'. He's always afraid I'm going to make the character too tough and too unapproachable for an audience. So we were down to a few scenes and he was nakedly now saying to me, 'Hey, I want you to cry in this movie'. Now that's one thing, as an actor, you never say. You don't go for an emotion – or one doesn't if they work the way I do. And this is the last kind of direction you want to hear."[26]

Instead of crying on cue, Nicholson decided to let the monologue take him to whatever emotional depths happened to surface. He's commented that the scene was a personal revelation. "On take one, away I went. And I think it was a breakthrough. It was a breakthrough for me as an actor, for actors. I don't think they'd had this level of emotion, really, in almost any male character until that point."[27] Following Jeff Corey's grounding in the Stanislavsky method, Nicholson resorted to "emotion memory" here for one of the few times in his career, thinking of his (grand) father's struggle with alcoholism and ultimately, cancer.

This received wisdom is all well and good but given what we know and feel about the elements of masquerade in Bobby's previous responses to emotive pressures, why should we suddenly take seriously this monologue simply because it appears to touch on the very core of the primal Oedipal conflict? Why shouldn't sensitivity be read as just another role in the repertoire? This is a largely dissenting view, but *Time Magazine* critic Jay Cocks, for one, felt the scene somehow fell short for these very reasons: "The scene does not fully work because Nicholson still has himself in check. There seems to be a point both for actor and character beyond which a sudden self-awareness cannot trespass, a hard and untouchable reserve."[28] On the other hand, one can also argue that all this somehow seems to fit, that Nicholson has intuited that his role as actor, as star, and Bobby's role as "son" are effectively the same. Both are aware that Bobby is in some ways "faking it", trying on the role of musician, like a costume, simply because it's expected as his father's son. He's been trying on different roles ever since, the contrite son not the least of his successes. Although far from any contemporary woman's idea of a feminist, Joan Riviere, for one, would probably have been proud.

# NOTES

1. Jack Nicholson, in Ron Rosenbaum, "Acting: The Method And Mystique Of Jack Nicholson", *The New York Times Magazine*, July 13, 1986, p.15.

2. Steve Erickson, "The Myth That Jack Built", *Esquire*, Vol. 114 No.3, September 1990, p.168.

3. Ibid, p.170.

4. "I like to play people that haven't existed yet, a future something, a cusp character. I have that creative yearning." Jack Nicholson, in Rosenbaum, op cit, p.16.

5. Cited in Patrick McGilligan, *Jack's Life: A Biography Of Jack Nicholson*, New York and London: W.W. Norton & Co., 1994, p.205.

6. See Robert David Crane and Christopher Fryer, *Jack Nicholson: Face To Face*, New York: M. Evans and Co., Inc, 1975, p. 23.

7. Robert B. Ray, *A Certain Tendency Of The Hollywood Cinema, 1930-1980*, New Jersey: Princeton University Press, 1985, p.260.

8. Eastman had known Nicholson since the late 1950s when both attended Jeff Corey's acting classes in Los Angeles. She later worked as scenarist on Monte Hellman's existential western, **The Shooting** (1965) – which also starred Nicholson – worked uncredited on Richard Lester's **Petulia** (1968) and scripted Jerry Schatzberg's **Puzzle Of A Downfall Child** (1970). See Jay Boyer, Bob Rafelson: *Hollywood Maverick*, New York: Twayne Publishers, 1996, p.36.

9. **Five Easy Pieces** was followed by the equally groundbreaking **The King Of Marvin Gardens** (1972); a torpid remake of James M. Cain's hardboiled classic **The Postman Always Rings Twice** (1981); and the largely forgettable commercial projects, **Man Trouble** (1992) and **Blood And Wine** (1996).

10. Boyer, op cit, p.xi.

11. "I don't try to give you an understanding of the people in a flick – just a description," says Rafelson. "Some flicks give you the essence. I want to give you the contradictions to the essence." Ibid, p.22.

12. Rafelson, in Kristine McKenna, "Return Of An Older, Wiser Bob Rafelson", *Los Angeles Times Calendar*, 28 September, 1986, p.21, cited in ibid, p.12.

13. Interpellated in Louis Althusser's sense of being "hailed" into ideology by the Symbolic Order.

14. Cited in McGilligan, op cit, p.229.

15. Erickson, op cit, p.172.

16. Beverly Walker, "The Bird Is On His Own: Jack Nicholson Interviewed", *Film Comment*, Vol.21 No.3, May-June, 1985, p.53.

17. Dennis Bingham, *Acting Male: Masculinities In The Films Of James Stewart, Jack Nicholson, And Clint Eastwood*, New Brunswick, New Jersey: Rutgers University Press, 1994, p.5.

18. "Womanliness therefore could be assumed and worn as a mask, both to hide the possession of masculinity and to avert the reprisals expected if she was found to possess it – much as a thief will turn out his pockets and ask to be searched to prove that he has not the stolen goods. The reader may now ask how I define womanliness or where I draw the line between genuine womanliness and the 'masquerade'. My suggestion is not, however, that there is any such difference; whether radical or superficial, they are the same thing." Joan Riviere, "Womanliness As A Masquerade", in Victor Burgin, James Donald and Cora Kaplan, eds., *Formations Of Fantasy*, London & New York: Methuen, 1986, p.38.

19. Bingham, op cit, p.101.

20. This connection between Nicholson and Brecht is not as far-fetched as it might seem. Nicholson's acting teacher Jeff Corey had himself learned acting in the Group Theatre and from the Yiddish Theatre actor (and later director), Jules Dessin before co-founding the Actors Lab in the late 1940s. Unlike many of his peers, Corey was not schooled in the Method but instead learned the Delsarte chart, which dated from the turn of the century and "which demonstrated the appropriate gesture for either an emotional, physical or mental condition." Rather than mechanize or ritualize the Method, Corey appropriated elements from Brecht and Peter Brook in addition to Stanislavsky and Lee Strasberg, stressing improvisation and playfulness and sudden bursts of anger to produce the required audience estrangement, all of which are Nicholson trademarks. See Pat McGilligan, "Corey-ography", *Film Comment*, Vol.25 No.6, November-December, 1989, p.39.

21. Jamie Wolf, "It's All Right, Jack", *American Film*, Vol.IX No.4, January-February, 1984, p.36.

22. Bingham, op cit, p.101.

23. "Even in first-rate performances, even as early as **Five Easy Pieces**, the persona intimidated the role. Truthfully, did you really buy him as a classical pianist?" Erickson, op cit, p.170.

24. Cited in McGilligan, *Jack's Life*, op cit, p.210.

25. Nicholson, in Rosenbaum, op cit, p.18.

26. Ibid, pp.18-19.

27. Ibid, p.19.

28. Jay Cocks, "The Star With The Killer Smile", *Time*, 12 August, 1974, p.47.

# 'CHINATOWN'

Jack Nicholson's performance as private detective J.J. Gittes in Roman Polanski's 1974 film **Chinatown** brought him on to the Hollywood A-List of romantic leading men for the first time. It established him as a big-time movie star who could command not only a large salary but also a new measure of critical and popular respect for his acting abilities. Most reviewers praised Nicholson's portrayal of the cynical, savvy, but ultimately defeated Gittes in Polanski's homage to *film noir*. The film itself was a commercial and critical hit because of a happy synergy created by a receptive national zeitgeist, an intelligent script by Robert Towne, brilliant direction by Roman Polanski, and a strong cast. This included not only Nicholson, but also Faye Dunaway as Gittes's client and lover Evelyn Mulwray, and legendary *film noir* director John Huston as crooked millionaire Noah Cross.

    **Chinatown** was Paramount producer Robert Evans' first film under his own production label. Evans hired screenwriter Robert Towne, who had previously written **The Last Detail**, to finish a detective-genre script Towne had been working on. Evans, wanting a starring vehicle for his then-wife Ali McGraw (who was about to run off with actor Steve McQueen), also thought of Jack Nicholson for the lead. For his script, Towne looked back into Los Angeles film and social history for inspiration. Sociologically, he was fascinated by the turn-of-the-century oil and water exploration and exploitation (by the likes of William Mulholland) upon which Los Angeles was built. Artistically, Towne was influenced by the hard-boiled detective stories of Raymond Chandler and Dashiel Hammett[1]. Director Polanski emphasized this aspect of the script during the extended re-write and simplification period[2].

    Ultimately, **Chinatown** became both neo-*film noir* and a fictionalized account of the Owen River Valley scandal in 1908. The man who unravels this torturous civic and personal mystery is Jake (J.J.) Gittes, whose profession and cynical wit are self-consciously crafted throwbacks to the iconic Bogartesque detectives of film past. Yet Gittes is also a departure from that past. Michael Eaton elaborates:

*Unlike Chandler's hero [Philip Marlowe], Jake is not a lone wolf located in a scummy Hollywood rented Office, he doesn't take his liquor from a cheap half-pint secreted in his filing cabinet and he doesn't look down his nose on divorce cases – they are mother's milk and father's meat and drink to him.*[3]

Peter Thompson adds: "Nicholson's character... was in the mold of a smartened-up Humphrey Bogart, smoother and less inclined to talk from the side of his mouth, though still rather monosyllabic". Initially, Gittes is hired

by a woman to investigate what he thinks he will be a fairly routine affair between his new client's husband, Hollis Mulwray, and another woman. However, when the real Mrs. Mulwray shows up and her husband (an important official with the city water authority) is found murdered, Gittes realizes he has been set up and doggedly proceeds to find out why. The Mrs. Mulwray imposter, a woman named Ida Sessions, is also murdered. At the end of the journey, Gittes discovers truth but no justice. He uncovers the representative of civic corruption, Noah Cross, but is unable to have him arrested. Cross is a man who purposefully manipulates the water supply of drought-stricken Los Angeles so that he and his cronies can buy up parched land from desperate farmers at low prices and become multi-millionaires.

As Gittes finally discovers, Cross is even more monstrous in his private life. He sleeps with his daughter, Evelyn Mulwray, and kills his son-in-law when Hollis attempts to prevent Cross from continuing his sexual poachings. The incestuous relationship has produced a child, Katherine, who is both Cross's daughter and granddaughter. At the film's climax, Evelyn – under duress – confesses the secret horror in her life: "[Katherine's] my sister. She's my daughter. My sister, my daughter... She's my sister and my daughter!... My father and I, understand?" Gittes's efforts to save Evelyn and Katherine from Cross are in vain. The film ends with Evelyn's accidental death by police gunfire and Gittes's failure in **Chinatown**. Though only one scene actually takes place in Chinatown itself, the district is nevertheless symbolically important as the place where Gittes in his former career as a cop "had learned that its inhabitants ran their own culture and that any outside interference brought only silence and shadows"[4].

Nicholson is perfectly cast as Jake Gittes – not surprisingly, since the part was more or less directly tailored to him. Towne created the character's memorable name from an amalgam of his nickname for Nicholson and the last name of a mutual friend named Harry Gittes[5]. This sharing of names is not the only cross-fertilization between fiction and the particulars of Nicholson's personal life that enhances the film's verisimilitude. Nicholson based Gittes's sartorial style on his father's example (although ironically, in light of the film's theme, the man Nicholson always thought was his father wasn't actually his father, though Nicholson wouldn't formally discover this until after **Chinatown** was completed). Also, during production, Nicholson's relationship with actress Angelica Huston – the daughter of co-star John Huston – lent an uncomfortable subtext to the scene in which Noah Cross interrogates Gittes about his relationship with Evelyn Mulwray ("are you sleeping with her?"). In Nicholson's own words: "I had just started going with John Huston's daughter, which the world might not have been aware of but it could actually feed the moment-to-moment reality of my scene with him"[6].

Finally, within the symbolic family headed by the director as *pater familias*, tensions on the set between Polanski and the two main cast members (Nicholson and Dunaway) may have actually enhanced the film's moody, edgy atmosphere. As most chroniclers of the film's production have noted, Dunaway and Polanski constantly complained about one another and had several verbal confrontations. Though Polanski and Nicholson were personal friends and remained on good terms throughout most of the production, they too had one famous blow-up. On the last day of filming, Polanski smashed Nicholson's dressing room TV as Nicholson left an unfinished scene to watch a basketball game between the New York Knicks and Nicholson's beloved Los Angeles Lakers. Later that day, Polanski and Nicholson reconciled. However, knowledge of the incident (and the on-set tensions that must have contributed to its violence) gives a note of disturbing authenticity to the scene in which Polanski's brutal thug slits open Gittes's nose.

In the physically and emotionally battered character of Gittes, Nicholson perfectly fused the countercultural intellectualism of his earlier screen roles with the slick physical presence of the traditional Hollywood leading man in a glossy, big-budget, commercial film. David Downing identifies the "early" Nicholson (as opposed to the "comfortable" Nicholson of the 1980s and '90s) as the best of a new breed of screen heroes. These characters combine old-fashioned individual charisma (or "star power") with a contemporary acknowledgement of the dehumanizing power and reach of the modern state:

*[The new hero] had to represent a blend of success and failure, an awareness that the latter was implicit in the former in modern America. Since the state was all-powerful, he had to recognize that the political and personal realms could not be brought together successfully... Nicholson, more than any other actor in the seventies, was to bring this truly new hero to fruition.*[7]

Such a fusion of contraries is present in the best of Nicholson's previous performances, such as **Easy Rider** (1969) and **Carnal Knowledge** (1971). However, **Chinatown** introduced Nicholson to a wider audience than ever and enhanced his reputation among those who already knew of his work. Producer Robert Evans elaborates:

*[**Chinatown**] establishes him as a major box-office star, which he hadn't been until **Chinatown** came out. He was an important critical star, and he had his coterie of fans, but now **Chinatown** is a breakthrough picture... he's so good as a leading man, as a romantic leading man. He's up there with everybody else who's a romantic leading man.*[8]

Critics such as Vincent Canby in *The New York Times* lauded Nicholson: "among the good things in **Chinatown** are... the performance by Nicholson, who wears an air of comic, lazy, very vulnerable sophistication that is the film's major contribution to the genre"[9]). Joseph Gelmis in *Newsday* compared Nicholson favourably to Humphrey Bogart and said "Jack Nicholson is one of the few actors in America today who can... get away with it"[10]. Michael Korda said unequivocally in *Glamour* that "Jack Nicholson... is quite simply one of the best actors in America today"[11]. Following the film's success and these kinds of notices, Nicholson went on to become a major Hollywood icon. He soon reaped the social and financial rewards of his success and won two Best Actor Academy Awards (for **One Flew Over The Cuckoo's Nest** in 1975 and **As Good As It Gets** in 1997), and one Best Supporting Actor Academy Award (for **Terms Of Endearment** in 1983).

Nicholson's audience appeal is a complex phenomenon that defies ready definition. He made his critical reputation by playing characters who subverted traditional American society, and yet in the past two decades, through personal lifestyle and selection of self-parodic film roles, has come to represent the narcissistic wealth of that entrenched system more than any other major Hollywood star[12]. He frequently dares to portray unattractive characters, yet consistently maintains audience sympathy. He is not conventionally handsome, yet his status as a Hollywood romantic leading man (both on-screen and off) is legendary. His screen persona cannot be definitively pinned down either. He can play manic villain and questing hero with equal plausibility. Roughly a decade of high-profile, over-the-top performances have ensured his bona-fides as "the heavy" (an axe murderer in **The Shining** [1980], Satan himself in **The Witches Of Eastwick** [1987], a gangster-turned-homicidal-artist in **Batman** [1989], and a hot-tempered Marine colonel in **A Few Good Men** [1992]). For other viewers, Nicholson is best remembered for films such as **Easy Rider** and **Cuckoo's Nest** as the alienated, rebellious, and ultimately martyred countercultural hero of the 1960s and early- to mid-1970s. Others might see him as the acerbic but loveable romantic hero of **Terms Of Endearment** and **As Good As It Gets**; conversely, he can convincingly play the romantic cad (in films like **Carnal Knowledge** and **Heartburn**). Some point to his portrayals of well-known historical figures such as playwright Eugene O'Neill in **Reds** (1981) and union leader Jimmy Hoffa in **Hoffa** (1992) as evidence of his range of talent. Still others praise his nuanced interpretations of morally ambiguous characters in dramas such as **The Last Detail** (1973), **The Postman Always Rings Twice** (1981), and **Prizzi's Honor** (1985). Nicholson's success in reinventing himself (or "selling out," as some might call it) as a major film star throughout thirty years of cultural change is attributable in part to his willingness to take on such a wide variety of roles.

However, most central to Nicholson's longevity as a star is his unique method of physically transforming himself into what Dennis Bingham labels "a spectacle of masculinism... [or] a set of assumptions about mastery and superiority[13]". The result upon the audience, if one may speak of the "typical" Nicholson performance, is to create within the spectator an ironic distance or alienation from the spectacle of character. From that abstracted distance, the spectator can then read the character as a personified commentary upon ideological and cultural constructions of masculinity in particular and contemporary society in general. Nicholson's acting, which increasingly tends to be heavily stylized in terms of physical mannerisms and facial expression and far from the naturalistic approach of his youthful roles, calls attention to its very artifice and widens the traditionally intimate identification between star and viewer.

The slightly "unreal" effect of the Nicholson character (especially his later ones, which sometimes verge on self-parody) is further enhanced by his signature physical attributes such as the nasal voice, the sinister but dazzling smile, the narrow eyes and triangular eyebrows, and the receding hairline. These features are consistently carried over from role to role, usually undisguised by make-up or hairpieces and paradoxically fashioning an easily recognizable mask that Nicholson places upon each of his characters. Douglas Brode takes note of that mask: "Jack's not so much a latter day man of a thousand faces, hiding a single characterization behind endless masks, as he is a man able to make a single face express a thousand personalities"[14]. The mask can most accurately be described as that of the embattled male in what Brode calls a probably futile life-search for an underlying "true" identity. This two-tiered search also typically involves a conflict with "an actual family or a substitute one, very often with a focus on a turbulent relationship with a father or foster-father figure"[15]. Brode observes that Nicholson – most likely as a result of his own illegitimate birth and the elaborate family charade that did not formally reveal this truth to him until his mother died in 1975 – seems drawn to roles where duality of character or identity is intimately associated with an ultimately fatal family conflict. Patrick McGilligan, in one of Nicholson's biographies, obliquely acknowledges the parallels between the fact of Nicholson's life and the fiction of Towne's screenplay: "The [Nicholson] family tree is a mystery with as many false clues as **Chinatown**"[16]. Thus, it is appropriate that Nicholson's breakthrough into superstardom came with the role of private detective J.J. Gittes, whose search for truth and redemption ends in the death of his lover and the bleak disaster of a terrible family secret revealed.

Gittes, as played by Nicholson, initially masks his inner desperation and emptiness with an urbane detachment from his squalid surroundings. The film opens by contrasting Gittes' calm demeanour with a client's howls of pain after Gittes has revealed photographs of the client's wife in an adulterous relationship with another man. In this opening scene, the film announces its intention to lay bare the secret sins of family life through the investigative techniques of the central character, Gittes. However, Gittes will be forced to abandon his professional detachment (exhibited in the opening scene with his client) as he becomes emotionally involved with a female client, Evelyn Mulwray. Gittes finds it increasingly more difficult to keep his professional mask in place as the personal demons of his past confront the present-day monsters of civic corruption, corporate greed, and family trauma. Nicholson finely calculates his performance to gradually pull away that mask and make clear to the audience the essence of Gittes's divided character.

Gittes as a character displays many dualities. He is at once hostile and kind; distant and committed; cynical and idealistic; jaded and romantic; vain and sloppy; sophisticated and vulgar; sleazy and noble; foolish and dignified; strong and vulnerable. Given the tragic vision that structures the film, Gittes is the perfect ambiguous hero (or anti-hero). His search to uncover the mystery behind the death of Hollis Mulwray is a quest that succeeds in revealing corruption but fails to redeem the society or individuals involved.

Gittes, in spite of his initial cockiness and seeming competence as a traditionally macho private detective, is unable to purge or punish the social evil he discovers, let alone rescue Evelyn Mulwray from it. The film's moral, to the extent that there is one, is spoken by Gittes's associate Walsh after Evelyn has died at the hands of Gittes's former police colleague: "Forget it, Jake. It's Chinatown."

In the metaphoric terms established by the film, the Chinatown district of Los Angeles is a hostile and morally ambiguous realm where Gittes as a cop unintentionally contributed to the death of a woman he loved and where his personal tragedy is doomed to repeat itself with Evelyn's shooting. Chinatown, as the film's symbol for the "moral and ethical quicksand in which modern society is sinking"[17], is also an objective correlative for the confused and powerless state of Gittes's mind when confronted by the corruption at the end of his journey. Most critics agree that the film's bleak resolution reflects in microcosm the American mood of the mid 1970s, when the Watergate scandal and threatened oil shortages capped off a decade and a half of political disillusionment. Screenwriter Towne's original ending was far more uplifting, in that Evelyn escapes her father by shooting him, but

Polanski's decision to end the film with Evelyn's death and Gittes's failure seems much more appropriate, given the times. Nicholson's ability to portray anxious vulnerability side-by-side with the iconic mannerisms of traditional masculinity makes him the perfect post-Bogart, post-Watergate detective hero for such a dark film.

Through Nicholson's performance, the film subverts the Hollywood-created myth of the private eye, or urban hero (John Cawelti and Richard Slotkin, among others, have written insightfully on this archetype). One of the most obvious characteristics of this heroic archetype is his rough-edged but nevertheless very real sophistication. He is able to take the measure of, or "read", nearly any social situation he finds himself in. Consequently, he can act in such a way as to obtain desired information or actions from the people he meets. He is also able to seduce women at will, both for personal pleasure and to further his investigation. Thus, he exploits and manipulates his fellow city-dwellers, but in the narrative terms established by the genre, he has only bested them at their own game. He finally does so not for selfish gain but in the pursuit of the higher goal of truth.

Nicholson's Gittes both exists within and mocks this heroic tradition of sophistication. The narcissistic Gittes always calculates ways in which to enhance his professional reputation. For one thing, he's a stylish dresser and even a bit of a dandy. Gittes's "look" is a transformation from the rather shabby, overcoated appearance of most genre private eyes. He spends most of the film in expensive suits, even while snooping about seacoasts and reservoirs. In spite of his own blue-collar origins and those of many of his clients (such as the fisherman Curly), he goes to great lengths to make his office as coolly cream-coloured and elegant as his clothing. He becomes agitated when the distraught Curly damages the office's physical appearance ("all right, Curly, enough's enough. You can't eat the venetian blinds. I just had 'em installed on Wednesday"). Gittes's concern with appearances even extends to his client list. His practice caters to the burgeoning Hollywood community of the 1930s, an association that makes Gittes himself, in the words of his barber, "practically a movie star". As part of his "movie star" persona, Gittes has also refined his sexual appeal so that his affair (obligatory in this genre) with the beautiful widow Evelyn seems inevitable. The on-screen affair also sparked rumours of a simultaneous real-life affair between Nicholson and Dunaway[18], demonstrating again the extent to which Nicholson's quirky glamour carries over to his fictional characters and vice versa.

However, the film consistently undermines Gittes (and Nicholson) as a glamorous figure. In spite of his pretensions toward the cultivation of wealth and sophistication, especially in his relations with the opposite sex, Gittes often reverts to crude or even violent behaviour quite at odds with his social aspirations but more in keeping with the private eye archetype. At the trivial level, his cackling delight in telling the long dirty joke about "screwin' like a Chinaman" to Walsh and Duffy embarrasses him in front of the elegant Evelyn Mulwray, who unbeknownst to him has heard the entire joke. More significantly, his frustration with Evelyn's stubborn secrecy and his own legal jeopardy later in the film causes him to erupt into a rage where he brutally slaps her until she confesses her incestuous relationship with her father. A few scenes later, when Gittes goes to his client Curly's house under false pretences to enlist Curly's help in escaping Lt. Escobar and is greeted at the door by Curly's bruised wife, Gittes's abuse of Evelyn is paralleled with Curly's off-screen beating of his unfaithful spouse. The alliance between the elegant private eye and the crudely physical fisherman, combined with their vicious beating of women, establishes both as patriarchal victimizers whose egocentric need for control leads them to violent excesses of temper. Dennis Bingham also makes the point that, since Gittes is the focus of every scene in the film, "the spectator becomes trapped into accepting Jake's lower middle class white male perceptions, perceptions that might approximate a spectator's own"[19]. Nicholson, ever since his role as the lawyer-turned-rebel in **Easy Rider**, has excelled in eliciting this kind of masculine identification while simultaneously drawing attention to its structural weaknesses.

Gittes's loss of psychological control is mirrored by periodic blows to his physical integrity and vanity. Early in Jake's investigation, Polanski's knife-wielding thug – after cornering him (with the help of others) against the fence at the reservoir – slashes his nose open. For much of the film, Gittes's injury requires him to wear a series of grotesque facial bandages – quite literally, masks – that are not only a visual metaphor of Gittes's duality of character but also a direct affront to his pride of appearance and male potency[20]. Nicholson's willingness to obscure his face in this manner still draws much favourable comment from critics, who praise his seeming lack of vanity. The bandage only comes off shortly before he makes love with Evelyn, tempting one to conclude that in this tender moment of connection Gittes has at last reconciled the opposites in his character. However, the stitched scar remains on his face as a visible reminder of his physical vulnerability and symbolic castration.

This point is made explicit when Loach, Escobar's partner, asks Gittes if someone slammed a bedroom window on his cut nose and Gittes wisecracks: "No, your wife got excited. She crossed her legs a little too quick." In reference to this scene, Michael Eaton says that Gittes is "concretising the phallic symbolism of his wound"[21]. As a fellow who sticks his nose into other people's business for a living, Gittes's nose literally becomes the emblem of his masculine power, or phallus. When the thug cuts him, the "nosy fellow" Gittes is emasculated and remains so for the rest of

the film. The nose-slashing scene reveals that Gittes, for all of his swagger, is easily rendered helpless and bloody by his more powerful enemies. In this, he's quite unlike his pugilistic cinematic ancestors who decisively beat up their adversaries and recover from bruises and cuts by the next scene. As an actor whose body is not so much the spectacular focus of viewer attention as his voice and eyes, a point made by Dennis Bingham[22], Nicholson is a good choice to lend "authenticity" to a supremely competent character who nevertheless fails by traditional masculine definitions at every turn.

Gittes is singularly vulnerable to beatings by crowds of men, as the film's story arc proves on several occasions. For example, as he drives through an orange grove, angry farmers mistake him for either an official of the water department or a real-estate developer, fire upon him, drag him from his wrecked car, beat him, and empty his pockets. His much-abused nose is again bloodied, and he's knocked unconscious. Only in the one-on-one fight with Sheriff Mulvihill (Cross's personal enforcer in the law enforcement community) at the Mar Vista Rest Home does Gittes prevail in traditional heroic fashion. When the rest of Mulvihill's thugs show up in the rest home parking lot (led by the sinister man whom earlier slashed Gittes's nose), Gittes wisely flees the scene in Evelyn's car. Complementing the film's anti-heroic theme of non-involvement, Gittes finds through his series of beatings that flight, rather than physical confrontation, is his best recourse. Nicholson's brand of machismo, while still redolent of the traditional masculine ethos, turns out to be quite hollow, since it is carried through his expressions and voice rather than his "hard body".

The film also subverts Gittes's idealistic pride in his seedy work. For example, right after Gittes's barber calls him a "movie star", a banker in the barbershop verbally attacks Gittes and his profession as private detective. "Listen, pal," Gittes's replies defensively. "I make an honest living. People only come to me when they're in a desperate situation. I help 'em out. I don't kick families out of their houses like you bums down at the bank do." However, Gittes's defense rings hollow, since his work as an investigator of infidelity and family secrets strikes right at the emotional core of home life. Also, as Michael Eaton observes, the barbershop scene introduces the "screwin' like a Chinaman" joke, which is in essence a racist tale about sexual infidelity that Gittes, by virtue of his daily work, finds uproariously funny[23]. However, when Gittes maniacally relays the off-colour joke to Walsh and Duffy back at the office – despite their efforts to stop him – Evelyn Mulwray overhears him. Jake is deeply embarrassed and unsettled by his social gaffe. His discomfort sets the tone for the rest of his disruptive professional (and personal) relationship with Evelyn – a relationship whose disastrous end illustrates the inherent destructiveness of Gittes's job.

In a later scene, the blind spots in Gittes's moral vision, originating in his background in law enforcement, are made very clear. When he believes he has been duped, he is incapable of seeing any other explanation of the facts of the case than the official police theory. When Lt. Escobar accuses Gittes of helping Evelyn cover up the murder of her husband, Gittes angrily says that Escobar is dumber than he looks. Eaton comments that "Jake bristles at the charge of extortion: it's where he draws the line, a type of venality beyond the bounds of his albeit flexible moral code"[24]. Gittes's own theory is that Hollis was killed by someone who found out the city was dumping water into the ocean, but when he discovers Hollis's spectacles in a salt-water pool in the yard of the Mulwray mansion, he comes to agree with Escobar. Angry and betrayed, he confronts and slaps Evelyn until she reveals to him that he and Escobar are both wrong in their theory about the murder. Gittes's moral outrage has been based upon false assumptions. His certainty in his own competence completely crumbles. All he can do now is try to stave off complete defeat for Evelyn – a task for which he isn't suited. Nicholson conveys Gittes's transformation from manic crusader to stunned onlooker with the stripping away of the cockiness from his physical bearing and the nasal edge from his voice.

Another of the standard characteristics of the traditional "hard-boiled" detective is his commitment to individual integrity and principle within a corrupt world. By comparison with the social system, the private detective, however socially disreputable, usually proves to be the one authentic agent of morality whose unique profession, both inside and outside the world of law enforcement, allows him to effect vigilante justice in the interests of a higher ethical truth. Nicholson's portrayal of Gittes both evokes this Hollywood archetype and topples it. According to Gittes's revelation to Evelyn shortly before they make love, the best advice he received while working as a beat cop in Chinatown was to "do as little as possible". When the film opens, Gittes has been doing just that. He's quit his career with the LAPD, renounced his youthful idealism, and gone to work as a private investigator specializing in squalid divorce cases. The seediness of his daily work enables him to maintain a safe distance from it, and from unsavoury clients such as the abusive husband Curly. Thus, Gittes is at once able to exercise his investigative talents and repress his futile outrage in the face of injustice. Throughout the first several scenes of the film, where Gittes and his associates Walsh and Duffy routinely tail Hollis Mulwray, Nicholson skilfully conveys the duality of Gittes's need for the process of police work alongside his personal detachment from its execution. Nevertheless, events inevitably conspire to involve Gittes personally in the Mulwray case.

First, the false Mrs. Mulwray (actually a woman named Ida Sessions employed by Noah Cross), turns the seemingly incriminating photographs that Gittes has taken of Hollis Mulwray and a young blonde woman (actually

Katherine) over to the newspapers. This act precipitates a full-blown civic scandal and angers the real Mrs. Mulwray into suing Gittes for defamation of character. Thus, Gittes must continue his investigation for two compelling reasons, one idealistic and one practical: uncovering the truth and salvaging his professional reputation. In a crucial scene that takes place at the Mulwray mansion, he explains his motives behind his continuing investigation to Mrs. Mulwray:

"I'm not in business to be loved, but I am in business. And believe me, Mrs. Mulwray, whoever set your husband up set me up. LA's a small town, people talk. I'm just trying to make a living. I don't want to become a local joke... Somebody's gone to a lot of trouble here and lawsuit or no lawsuit, I intend to find out. I'm not supposed to be the one who's caught with his pants down."

Yet Gittes still maintains to Mrs. Mulwray that his investigation is "nothing personal". Mrs. Mulwray scoffs at this ("is this a business or an obsession with you?"). Gittes lets her question pass unremarked, but at this point in the film the viewer can answer the question for her: both. Gittes is simultaneously engaged in nothing more than an effort to clear his name for mundane financial reasons and nothing less than an all-out search for answers based on a traditional hero's private code of integrity.

In a later scene, after Gittes's nose has been slashed, he explains this same duality of motive to Mrs. Mulwray in even more explicit terms ("it seems like half the city is trying to cover [this case] all up, which is fine by me. But Mrs. Mulwray, I goddamn near lost my nose. And I like it. I like breathing through it. And I still think you're hiding something"). For these kinds of personal reasons, Gittes is determined to discover what his client is hiding. Nicholson carries such scenes as these with his inimitable blend of detached irony, expressed through the lazy voice, slightly mocking smile, and moral intensity, revealed in those famously narrow "cobra" eyes.

Gittes's confidence – even smugness – in his professional competence allows the viewer to trust him as the audience's agent in uncovering the mystery. Gittes knows all the tricks of his trade (for instance, leaving a pocket watch beneath the tire of Hollis's car so that when Gittes later retrieves the smashed watch he will know what time Hollis left). He possesses the necessary nerve and rhetorical skills to match wits with Noah Cross at the Albacore Club. But Gittes is mistaken all along in his theory about the case, and the audience is mistaken along with him. He's been used by both Evelyn and Noah in a domestic war over Katherine and has no idea why until the last few scenes. When he finally discovers the private truth behind the public swindle, his re-commitment to saving a threatened woman (in this case, Evelyn) is futile. Michael Eaton concludes:

*Jake's fate is to be forever stuck in liminality, knowing everything, having nothing. He is barely able to stand as he led into the enveloping darkness, condemned only to repeat... The story is all but over, the social order... is restored – but not to decency, rationality, love, health and meaning, but to a fundamental, chaotic, unconquerable and unembraceable perversity.*[25]

The final thematic pessimism of **Chinatown** is captured perfectly in Nicholson's anguished expression and defeated posture as Escobar releases him from custody and Walsh and Duffy carry him away from the scene of Evelyn's death.

In retrospect, it's little wonder that this film about water and corruption did so well in the year of Watergate. And although Nicholson didn't win an Oscar for **Chinatown**, his breakthrough role ensured that his public stardom and critical appeal, now merged into one phenomenon, would soon thereafter carry him victorious on to the stage at the Academy Awards. Much later in his career, Nicholson would attempt to return to the star-making character of Gittes in 1990's **The Two Jakes**, a film which he not only starred in but directed. The sequel was a disappointment, mostly because it lacked the thematic bite of Polanski's original. Nicholson as an established superstar in a materially comfortable middle age has also faced criticism that his performances have become overly stylized self-parodies of aging masculinity. However, the key element in Nicholson's stardom – his ability to "twist" traditional leading-man roles into at least the appearance of subversive irony – consistently endures.

# NOTES

1.  Patrick McGilligan, *Jack's Life: A Biography Of Jack Nicholson*, New York: W.W. Norton & Co., 1994:248.

2.  John Parker, *The Joker's Wild: The Biography Of Jack Nicholson*, London: Anaya Publishers, 1991:131.

3.  Michael Eaton, *Chinatown*, BFI Film Classics, London: British Film Institute, 1997:19.

4.  Donald Shepherd, *Jack Nicholson: An Unauthorized Biography*, New York: St. Martin's Press, 1991:102.

5.  McGilligan, 249.

6.  Cit. in Parker, 126.

7.  David Downing, *Jack Nicholson: A Biography*, New York: Stein & Day, 1984:66.

8.  Evans, cit. in Robert David Crane and Christopher Fryer, *Jack Nicholson: Face To Face*, New York: M. Evans and Company, 1975:122-3.

9.  Cit. in Norman Dickens, *Jack Nicholson: The Search For A Superstar*, New York: Signet, 1975:133.

10. Ibid.

11. Ibid.

12. See Dennis Bingham, *Acting Male: Masculinities In The Films Of James Stewart, Jack Nicholson And Clint Eastwood*, Rutgers UP, New Brunswick, NJ: 1994:149-59.

13. Bingham, 102.

14. Brode, 24.

15. Ibid., 25.

16. McGilligan, 32.

17. Barbara Siegel and Scott Siegel, *Jack Nicholson: The Unauthorized Biography*, New York: Avon, 1990:73.

18. Nancy Campbell, *Jack Nicholson*, Greenwich, CT: Brompton Books, 1994:37.

19. Bingham, 133.

20. Ibid., 129.

21. Eaton, 59.

22. Bingham, 151.

23. Eaton, 30-31.

24. Ibid., 59.

25. Ibid., 71.

# PRESENCE AS ABSENCE: JACK NICHOLSON IN 'THE PASSENGER'

*"The whole film is ambiguous, but I think that it appropriates such ambiguity as its own concreteness."*[1]

In 1974, the year that anticipated the results of his collaboration with Michelangelo Antonioni, the release of **The Last Detail** and **Chinatown** confirmed Jack Nicholson's star status just as they reinforced his reputation as one of the finest actors of his Hollywood generation. Indeed, in that one short period of his career, from about 1972 to 1976, Nicholson had delivered, and was about to deliver, most of his landmark performances in films including **The King Of Marvin Gardens, One Flew Over The Cuckoo's Nest**, and even the underrated **The Missouri Breaks**. Right in the middle of this period both of unmatched creativity and increased professional power he chose to go to Europe to star in **The Passenger**, a small art film directed by an Italian who had a reputation for making films which set out to emphasise the artificiality of character and to highlight the distance between characters and audience. On the surface it seems like a curious choice to say the least, but Nicholson's choice of roles, while not always successful, had to this point mostly been brave, intelligent and idiosyncratic. Furthermore, and without wishing to labour the point, it is possible to draw connections between the actor's curious family background and the central theme of the film, the quest of his character for something like a meaningful identity.

Nicholson was brought up in what he assumed was a normal, relatively happy domestic environment with his parents and two older sisters. The fact that his supposed parents were actually his grandparents and that one of his "sisters" was in reality his mother who had born him outside of marriage and had colluded with the rest of the family in covering his bastardy up was only revealed to him in 1975, and the revelation shocked him deeply. Comments he made in interviews years before he found out the truth about his family imply that he may well have suspected that all was not as it seemed, and he admits that he harboured a strong antipathy towards family structures for a considerable period before 1975. In the context of this destabilising, almost perverse childhood situation, perhaps it is not altogether surprising that he was drawn to **The Passenger** and to the character of David Locke, who trades his identity on a whim and gives up his family and whose search for meaning provides the impetus for the film's narrative.

The film's plot, such as it is, opens with TV reporter David Locke on

assignment in Africa, trying to set up an interview with representatives of a guerilla army. The guerillas prove to be elusive and David becomes increasingly frustrated and feels increasingly isolated in the immensity of the African desert. An outsider, an observer with nothing concrete to observe, he is ignored by the locals and finds his only human contact in a fellow guest at his hotel. David's new friend, an Englishman by the name of Robertson, is in the country on unspecified business. One day, after yet another failed attempt to make contact with the guerillas, David returns to the hotel to find Robertson dead. The two men look very much alike and, apparently on a whim, David puts on Robertson's shirt and then changes the pictures in their passports. After persuading the hotel manager that it is David Locke who has died, David packs up all of Robertson's belongings and leaves to live his new life as the Englishman.

The film picks up David in London, where he spies on his own wife and child at their home as they are coming to terms with the fact of his (David's) death, a report of which is broadcast on TV. Next he travels to Germany and then to Spain, following leads based on appointments Robertson had to keep. As he travels, he picks up a young architecture student whose name we never learn (Maria Schneider) who travels with him.

Her motivations are hard to divine, although it seems as if her continual interest in his maintaining the identity of Robertson (an insistence which finally leads to his death) in some way grants her – or shores up – her own identity. As he travels in his new identity, David also learns that Robertson was no ordinary businessman – he was running guns to the guerilla forces David was himself trying to contact. In this way, the connection between the two men is reinforced, only with David recast from disinterested observer to protagonist.

At the same time, David's wife Rachel (Jenny Runacre) comes to suspect that something is amiss and resolves to locate Robertson who is reported to have been the last man to see David alive. Rachel follows David/Robertson across Europe almost running into him, but never quite managing to connect. David is also being followed by agents or representatives of the enemies of the guerillas Robertson was meant to provide with weapons and, when they finally catch up with him, they kill him. The film ends with David's wife looking at her husband's body and being questioned by the local police. "I never knew him", she observes, a line which the police assume refers to their dead man, "Robertson", but which the audience understands to refer as much if not more to her husband, David.

**Professione: Reporter (The Passenger / Fatal Exit**, 1974) is the third of three feature films the Italian director Michelangelo Antonioni made outside of his native Italy in the late 1960s and early 1970s. This period in Antonioni's career, beginning with his loose adaptation of Julio Cortazar's story "Las babas del diablo" [the devil's drool] as **Blow-up** (1966) can be argued to mark a distinct phase in the development of the director's long term engagement with the problem of fiction, of story telling. Although Antonioni's first films were documentaries, it is as a director of "estranged", often wilfully obtuse and abstracted feature films that he made his reputation. Indeed, by the time of **Il Deserto Rosso (Red Desert**, 1964), his last full feature before coming to London to make **Blow-up** with David Hemmings and Vanessa Redgrave, Antonioni had already been appropriated by many critics as a central proponent of that curious, contested phenomenon: "European art cinema".

For his part, Jack Nicholson, who acknowledges that he took the lead in **The Passenger** because he "...wanted to do an Antonioni movie," was, in so doing, following an understandable desire to work with directors whose work spoke to him and inspired him as well as being – at least by default – part of an ongoing process of bringing challenging European films to a wider American audience.[2]

That being said, it is important not to imply that there was, at the time, such a simple thing as a unified, consistent body of work that constituted European, to say nothing of art, cinema; and one would need to make distinctions between "schools" and movements with national origins as well as further distinctions within national cinemas in order to understand just what it was that Nicholson wanted to acknowledge – more, temporarily to become a part of – when he elected to work in Europe in the mid 1970s. One would need, for example, to make a distinction between the work of Italian directors such as Antonioni and Fellini who had not become known for working in the post-war Italian neo-realist style and other, neo-realist directors such as Rossellini, de Sica and the early Visconti.

The Italian critic, Lorenzo Cuccu's attempt to explicate this distinction has the benefit of encapsulating it in the function of the camera which had, for Antonioni (if not for the neo-realists) an active, interpolative part to play in the process of film making. As Cuccu writes, for Antonioni "...the cinematic operation is creative not because it reproduces a creatively elaborated material but for what it adds, in meaning and artistic elaboration, to this material."[3] In an interview with *The Guardian* in 1975, Antonioni himself offers a political interpretation of both (by implication) his distance from neo-realism and of his search for ambiguity and dissolution in the identities of his characters:

*"We have created a structure that suscitates doubts. We are all dissatisfied. The international situation, politically and otherwise, is so unstable, that the lack of stability is reflected within each individual. But I'm used to talking in pictures, not words. When I talk of man, I want to see his face. In China,* [Antonioni had shot a documentary **Chung Kuo: China**, 1972, in China before starting work on **The Passenger** and had been excoriated by the Chinese authorities for supposedly producing a piece of anti-communist propaganda, an accusation Antonioni strenuously denied] *when I asked them what was the thing they felt was most important in their revolution, they said it was the new man. That is what I tried to focus on. Each individual, each one creating his own little revolution, all those little revolutions which together will change humanity. That's why I insist upon a personal viewpoint, concretizing it with the camera; every change in history has always started from individuals. You can't change facts: it's the human mind that creates human action."[4]*

And yet, of course, Antonioni's understanding of "focusing on individuals" was very different from the Hollywood norm – even from the developing traditions of American independent cinema in the period. When Antonioni speaks of his motivation in making **The Passenger**, he does so from a perspective closer to that of an autobiographer than a conventional director:

*"It might seem strange for me to say this, but **Blow-up** was in some ways my neo-realist film on the relation between the individual and reality, even if it has a metaphysical component... After this film, I wanted to see what there was behind, what was my own appearance in the inside of myself, a little bit like I had done in my earliest films. And what resulted was **The Passenger**, another step forward in the study of contemporary man. In **Blow-up** the relationship between the individual and reality is perhaps the principal theme, while in **The Passenger**, the relation is the one of the individual with himself."*[5]

It is a perspective which has serious implications for the role of the actor and for the function of character within the film and is one which, arguably, has much to do with generating from Nicholson a performance which, at a surface level, is against type but which is somehow also, and in a distinctly personal way, very much in character. It is a performance which stands as his most natural, his least affected and, I would submit, in many ways his most accomplished to date. In order to put that performance in context; in order to understand what Antonioni wanted from Nicholson and, possible biographical connections aside, what might have drawn Nicholson out from the orbit of Hollywood one needs to see the alternative that Antonioni's exploratory, impressionistic film making offered.

Conventional approaches to film acting in the United States – the approaches underlying the training of actors at any rate – borrowed directly from theatrical traditions and were bound up in a whole set of assumptions regarding the nature of character and its function in drama. Outlining an established, theatre derived approach, the American drama coach, Lillian Albertson comments in her 1947 acting manual that: "...before performance comes interpretation. By that I mean the strictly intellectual analysis of a role."[6] Dramatic character, for Albertson, is something to be studied and understood. It is – at least in terms of the actor's duty and ability to circumscribe coherent and consistent motivation – both a bounded and a penetrable phenomenon.

We are familiar, in Britain and America, with the idea that a film actor's job is to produce the on-screen illusion of a well rounded character – an individual, whose "arc" or process of emotional development in the course of the film's narrative is, if nothing else, a marker for the audience of "realism", of identification and empathy which is simultaneously a central plot device. We also understand, even if unconsciously, that this display of growth and development has a directly political, one might say ideological content. We understand that there is a "work ethic" involved in this kind of drama. Our character needs to be seen to grow as a person in order to prove worthy of the success or happiness that the habitual closure of a Hollywood

film ensures him or her, and for that if for no other reason, that growth is played out specifically and necessarily as a function of plot.

One consequence of this attitude is the overriding value placed upon "authenticity", however defined, by many approaches to the training of actors (including the "Method", although its significance has been exaggerated). A particular approach to the preparation of a role becomes important for many actors, specifically immersion in the real world that the film will attempt to reconstruct as fiction. Of course Nicholson who had, incidentally, trained with Jeff Corey in Los Angeles, was working in this kind of framework in his American career. In preparing for his role as McMurphy in **One Flew Over The Cuckoo's Nest**, a film released within a year of **The Passenger**, Nicholson spent two weeks at the Oregon State Mental Hospital: "...where he persuaded hospital authorities to let him mingle with the most disturbed patients, eating in their mess halls and closely observing their speech patterns and bodily movements. He even watched patients undergoing the same shock treatments McMurphy would be subjected to in the film, in order to make his depiction more authentic."[7]

In the world of Antonioni's cinema the rules, such as they are, are different. Actors are deployed on the screen as figures in a landscape, bodies divorced from the everyday world. *Sight & Sound*'s contemporary reviewer relates theme to character and to mise en scène in **The Passenger** in terms of oppositions: "The theme of the film is not related to these figures in the landscape in the same direct way as in Antonioni's Italian pictures... There is in **The Passenger** a much less direct, less "expressive" relationship. In fact, the theme of the film – the search for identity, for commitment – is expressed only glancingly, by ironic contrast. The more closely Antonioni relates his characters to their physical environment, the more dissociated from it they seem to be." At the start of the film, for example, when Locke is focused upon his African assignment he is ignored by the population – memorably by a camel rider – and is lost in the incoherence of the political situation that he is supposed to be making sense of for the consumption of domestic television viewers. *Film Comment*'s reviewer suggests connections that work in terms of the imagery but which are as fleeting as light through the projector lens itself: "Waiting, expecting. Locke is nevertheless never met by anyone or anything except a fleeting romance, a few brief moments of flying over blue water, a few hours of travelling within a green and flowered paradise. Stuck in the desert, he is momentarily reborn, only to return speedily to the desert and death."

This is not to imply that Antonioni's characters have no quotidian identity, rather that the circumstances of the narrative lead to a separation, a slippage away from many of the concerns of ordinary life as Pierre Sorlin suggests: "...these fictional people were deprived of conscience, spectators did not watch the world through their eyes and were not informed of their state of mind... The characters in these films were not given an appearance of existence, they were kept aloof, silent, deprived of evident feelings, as if they only existed for and by way of the film camera."[8]

What remains when most of the surface clues to deeper interpretation are stripped away are actorly focus, interaction, and most importantly in the figure of Jack Nicholson, just as with Monica Vitti and other Antonioni performers before him, the indefinable *sine qua non* of stardom: *presence*. In the absence of more habitual topics for discussion, it is this last quality that has been foregrounded most frequently in journalistic and critical responses to Nicholson's acting in **The Passenger**. One contemporary critic puffs Nicholson's performance in just these terms: "Nicholson plays a resourceful man who has exhausted his resourcefulness with the easy eloquence that characterizes his acting. Since the early performances of Brando, no American screen actor has had Nicholson's almost hypnotic gift of being absolutely present. As with Brando, it is almost impossible to take your eyes from him, even when he seems to be doing nothing."[9]

It is, of course, delightfully ironic that the signal virtue here identified in praise of the performance of a character defined almost exclusively in terms of his metaphysical absence is the magnetism of the actor playing him. *Variety*'s critic in 1975 uses similar language to pre-empt his implied readers' inability to think too far out of their Hollywood box, writing of "...the commanding and resourceful performance of Jack Nicholson [who] ...plays the character with a personal flair, as penetrating as Antonioni's handling of the film." Gilliatt, as one might expect, does rather better, acknowledging the choices Nicholson makes and the physicality of his performance: "Nicholson's performance is a wonder of insight. How does he animate a personality that is barely there? He does it by cutting out nearly all the inflections from his voice, by talking very slowly, by making random movements. One particular gesture is oddly expressive and impassioned. A slight flapping of the arms, as if he were trying to fly."[10]

If critics were searching for a language to interpret Nicholson's work, Nicholson himself has difficulty accounting for the nature of his relationship with his director. He is not always entirely complimentary – it is clear that their on-set relationship was not without its challenges – but he acknowledges the personal commitment and control Antonioni brought to the project and he suggests that they got on as well as they did because the director saw a similar commitment in the work of his star:

*"Working with him is the outside pole of film idiosyncrasy. Once you've been through a production with Antonioni, no one is going to ever throw you with strange moves again. He's fully in control of what he's doing, but he really does it his own way. We'd probably still be shooting if he wasn't locked in by contracts. I mean, he lay down in front of the plane to keep Richard Harris from leaving Red Desert. The guy just kept shooting and shooting and shooting 'cause he loves making movies, and that's why he's great. He drives you crazy. The guy throws two tantrums a week. They tell me I'm the first actor in 25 years he got along with, but that was because I wanted to do an Antonioni movie."[11]*

Although in interviews Nicholson has tended to be somewhat gnomic about his reasons for choosing to work on **The Passenger**, it is clear that Antonioni's work inspired him. Of course the art house director also had recently verged on becoming hip with his recent vision of "Swinging London" in **Blow Up**. Whatever the reasons, the choice fits a period in which Nicholson had not done exploring opportunities to push his own boundaries. It is tempting, therefore, to think of his disciplined, spare performance in **The Passenger** as something of a negative twin to his McMurphy in **One Flew Over The Cuckoo's Nest**. Both parts took Nicholson to extremes; both involved a certain proximity to madness. The former brushed against the entropy that the film locates beneath the veneer of personality and socialisation; the latter explores the other limit of personality that is mania. Nicholson tried both extremes in the early 1970s. That he went on to model much of the rest of his career on the second frame is a matter for other contributions to this volume.

The experience of working with Antonioni certainly lingered as an imagistic, stylistic and even humorous frame of reference in Nicholson's mind after the film was finished. Talking to Andy Warhol's *Interview* magazine in 1976, he recounts an everyday incident when he got stuck in a lift with a group of friends. They had to get out in a cellar and found everything was locked and that there was no way out: "It was totally Antonioniesque," Nicholson recalls, "...the whole scene – just wandering around in this kind of cellar where it's concrete blocks, but painted with enamel in colours like light brown and butterscotch so it looked like a high fashion set, truly, more than anything else."[12] This, then, is the final, ironic reduction, the slipping away of the figure of Antonioni to landscape that Nicholson performs, just as the director performed the same effect on the actor a year or so before.

# NOTES

1. Michelangelo Antonioni in interview "Il Mondo è Fuori dalla Finestra" from *Filmcritica* 252, March 1975 (trans. Dana Renga).

2. Douglas Brode *The Films of Jack Nicholson* New Jersey: Citadel Press, 1987 p.164.

3. Lorenzo Cuccu Antonioni: *Il Discorso dello Sguardo: Da "Blow up" a "Identificazione Di Una Donna"* Pisa: ETS Editrice, 1990 p.21 (cited in: Peter Brunette *The Films Of Michelangelo Antonioni* Cambridge: Cambridge University Press, 1998 p.14).

4. Gideon Bachmann "Talking Of Michelangelo" *The Guardian* 18 February, 1975 (cited in: Carlo di Carlo & Giorgio Tinazzi (eds.) *Michelangelo Antonioni: The Architecture Of Vision: Writings And Interviews on Cinema* (American edition) New York: Marsilio Publishers, 1996 p.332). Antonioni also offers a clear statement of his position vis a vis neo-realism in the same interview: "I am *not* really a good son of neo-realism: I'm rather the black sheep of its family, and with this film [**The Passenger**] even more so I have replaced my objectivity with that of the camera. I can direct it any way I want: as the director, I am God. I can allow myself any kind of liberty. Actually, the liberty I have achieved in the making of this film is the liberty the character in the film tried to achieve by changing identity." p.330.

5. Cesare Biarese & Aldo Tassone *I film di Michelangelo Antonioni* Rome: Gremese Editore, 1985 pp.136-7 (cited in: Brunette p.126).

6. Lillian Albertson *Motion Picture Acting* New York: Funk & Wagnalls, 1947 p.65.

7. Brode p.187. I have written elsewhere about the impact of the method on American actors in the post war period (see *Dennis Hopper: Movie Top Ten* in the same series), but it is worth quoting Carnicke's conclusion to a paper assessing Strasberg's approach which highlights the paradoxical imperatives of this kind of work as a further illustration of the alternative that was Antonioni's practice: "Lee Strasberg's paradox for the actor is twofold. While promoting respect for the actor, he places the director in charge of performance. While stressing that natural behaviour is the stuff of acting, he trains the actor in practical techniques. On the one hand, he teaches actors to cope with the authority invested in the director by the power of montage. On the other hand, he creates ways in which the actor can cope with everyday conditions of film work that fragment, disrupt, and essentially deconstruct the experience of performing. In short, the two predominant commonplaces about the Method – that Strasberg changes Stanislavsky and that his students succeed most in film – are indeed inextricably linked." Sharon Marie Carnicke *Lee Strasberg's Paradox of the Actor* in Allan Lovell and Peter Krämer (eds.) *Screen Acting* London: Routledge, 1999 p.86.

8. Pierre Sorlin *Italian National Cinema 1896-1996* London: Routledge, 1996 pp.130/133.

9. Brode p.165.

10. Ibid p.165.

11. Ibid p.164.

12. *Interview* magazine 1976 p.24.

# 'ONE FLEW OVER THE CUCKOO'S NEST'

## ONE

Published in 1962, Ken Kesey's provocative novel *One Flew Over The Cuckoo's Nest* was based on his personal experiences of working as a night attendant on the psychiatric ward of the Veterans Hospital in Menlo Park. Kesey admitted to writing much of the book under the influence of LSD and other hallucinogens, as well as enduring electro-shock treatment in order to better describe the effects on mentally ill patients.

Before the book was published, veteran Hollywood character actor Kirk Douglas (fresh from being crucified in Stanley Kubrick's **Spartacus** [1960]) bought the rights to the text, believing it would make a successful film with himself in the lead role as Randle Patrick McMurphy, a charismatic but mentally disturbed sociopath just committed to the hospital. Testing the waters, Douglas would take the book and adapt it for Broadway with himself in the title role, but the production failed to fully capture the complex narrative and emotional themes expressed so forcefully in the book, and the play bombed. With the theatrical failure, Douglas was free to accept (a previously turned down) invitation from President John F. Kennedy to join him on a goodwill mission to Czechoslovakia.

In Prague, Douglas would meet the then largely unknown Milos Forman, then a thirty-one year old scriptwriter and director with the Prague Film faculty of the Academy of the Dramatic Arts. On his return home Douglas, impressed with his acquaintance, sent Forman a copy of *Cuckoo's Nest* with the hope that he would join him in the still planned film project. But, in a strange twist of fate, the package never arrived and Forman remained in Prague unaware that Douglas wanted to collaborate with him. Douglas would encounter further delays when the rights to the book became locked in a protracted legal battle between Douglas and his former partner in the Broadway production. Once the property became free again, Kirk Douglas's son Michael, now achieving critical recognition after his successful TV series *The Streets Of San Francisco*, showed an interest in getting the project produced for the screen.

With the rights to the book and a new, more contemporary screenplay written to express society's changing attitudes in the decade since the book's original publishing, Michael Douglas found the major studios disinterested in financing a film adaptation – his father's Broadway failure quoted as a reason for the reticence. Douglas looked elsewhere and finally approached Saul Zaentz, head of Fantasy Records, who was so taken with the book he agreed to finance most of the film, then budgeted at $4 million.

Zaentz and Douglas coincidentally soon approached Forman (who had now emigrated to the US), unaware that ten years earlier, Kirk Douglas had attempted to send him the book. With Forman on board (he had made **A Blonde in Love** [1967] and **The Fireman's Ball** [1971] in the intervening decade), after considering the then major box office star Burt Reynolds for the central protagonist McMurphy, Michael Douglas' attentions soon turned to Jack Nicholson, fresh from performances in Hal Ashby's **The Last Detail** ('74), Roman Polanski's **Chinatown** ('74) and Michelangelo Antonioni's **The Passenger** ('75).

Nicholson in his portrayal of R.P. McMurphy would play a brawler and convicted rapist who manages to convince the authorities that he is mentally disturbed in order to escape a heavy prison sentence. More complicated however, Nicholson would have to offer up a performance in McMurphy that whilst feigning insanity, would show his character was still possessed of a potent mental disorder of which he was unaware.

Nicholson flew up to the Oregon State Hospital in Salem (which would be the location for the film) during pre-production. The hospital had 582 inmates, most of whom were classed as criminally insane. While there, he had meetings with the Director of the hospital Dr Dean Brooks (who only agreed to the filming in his hospital after a commitment from producers Zaentz and Douglas that the film would not denigrate his patients), the nurses and some of the inmates. Personally persuading the hospitals medical chief, Nicholson was able to watch patients undergoing electric shock treatment before spending time in the maximum security ward to see the patients being brought out of their cells. Many of the inmates, believing Nicholson to be a new patient, were eager to engage him in conversation – and this included a young man who three weeks earlier had killed a prison warden with twenty-eight stab wounds.

Said Nicholson "There were all these mentally shattered, destroyed human beings about you. And I asked one of the orderlies 'How do you do this as a job?' There were people there that stabbed people, all kinds of horrible things. And he just looked me in the eye and said something I won't forget, 'Well, Jack, some people do get better.'"

Douglas and Forman in their quest for the perfect ensemble cast were to see up to 900 actors for the dozen principle roles. The cast would finally include a young Danny De Vito, Christopher Lloyd, Brad Dourif, Louise Fletcher as Nurse Ratched, McMurphy's nemesis (Fletcher chosen after Anne Bancroft, Jane Fonda and Faye Dunaway all turned down the role) and the unknown Will Sampson who played the Indian Chief Bromden.

# TWO

From the outset McMurphy has the air of a man who has spent a lifetime goading the order within the "establishment". Arriving at the hospital handcuffed, once inside the sterile and simplistically functional ward, where a structured, rigid calm prevails, McMurphy – after sizing up the physically towering Chief only to be told by another patient, the stuttering Billy Bibbit (Brad Dourif) that the Chief is deaf and dumb – immediately focuses on a small group of patients engrossed in their obviously haphazard and largely improvised game of poker. McMurphy disrupts the game between Billy, Martini (Danny De Vito), Cheswick (Sydney Lassick) and Harding (William Redfield) by producing a pack of playing cards of nude women, and Martini and Billy leave the game to follow McMurphy elsewhere.

The following scene finds McMurphy in the office of Dr Spivey (Dr Dean Brooks) where it is revealed that McMurphy has been committed for the rape of an underage girl and for numerous fights. Dr Spivey questions McMurphy about the reasons why he believes he has been committed to the hospital to which McMurphy provides vague and guarded answers before the narrative returns the film back to the ward and to a group discussion with Nurse Ratched, the moderator. The discussion focuses on Harding who has been having sexual problems with his wife and while McMurphy is content to keep quiet during this his first meeting, Harding's intellectualised and increasingly pretentious comments on the nature of man soon cause an animated verbal battle between a number of the group.

In the basketball court outside the ward, McMurphy attempts to teach the Chief how to play basketball in one of the film's more lighthearted sequences, before the film returns to the ward where McMurphy is holding fort over another game of poker. Annoyed that the music being piped into the ward by Nurse Ratched is overly loud, he attempts but fails to get her to turn the music down so that "some of the men can talk". His anger at losing this first encounter with Nurse Ratched and thus with the bureaucracy of the establishment, manifests itself in the following scene where during another group discussion, McMurphy proposes to Nurse Ratched that the rules in the ward be changed so that the patients can watch a game of the 1963 baseball World Series on the television. Nurse Ratched proposes this suggestion is put to a vote but only McMurphy and two other patients agree to the change. McMurphy realises that his fellow patients are both fearful of breaking the monotonous regime of the ward and of incurring the displeasure of Nurse Ratched. McMurphy chides his fellow patients for their perceived weaknesses.

Later that night, McMurphy tells his fellow inmates that he is going to break out of the hospital to visit a bar in the town to watch the baseball. They ridicule his idea, so McMurphy takes bets that he can lift a heavy shower unit and smash his way out. The patients watch spellbound as McMurphy, though giving it all, fails to life the unit from its base. Walking out of the room McMurphy responds "Well at least I tried Goddammit, at

least I tried".

The film returns to another group discussion where Billy has become the focus of the attention. A weak willed mama's boy, Billy's previous sexual experiences with a woman is used as a powerful psychological weapon against him by Nurse Ratched, who reminds him of his mother's entrenched and negative feelings on such matters. Billy is terrified by the mention of his mother but the topic of discussion is severed when McMurphy (now beginning to believe his masculine/aggressive nature at the ward is influencing the other inmates), again proposes to have another vote on changing the rules to watch a ball game. The entire discussion group agrees to the change but Nurse Ratched (with apparent barely concealed glee) reminds McMurphy of the remaining inmates (even though they are obviously substantially more mentally disturbed that the discussion group itself). McMurphy again fails to win over Nurse Ratched and the entrenched bureaucracy that prevails and, finally losing his temper, demands she turn on the television nevertheless.

When this fails to transpire, McMurphy suddenly "sees" the game on the television and begins his own running commentary. The rest of the group join him at the television and cheer along with him (though the TV is turned off). The implication of his actions is loaded with ambiguity – does McMurphy pretend the game is on, to both psychologically attack Nurse Ratched and

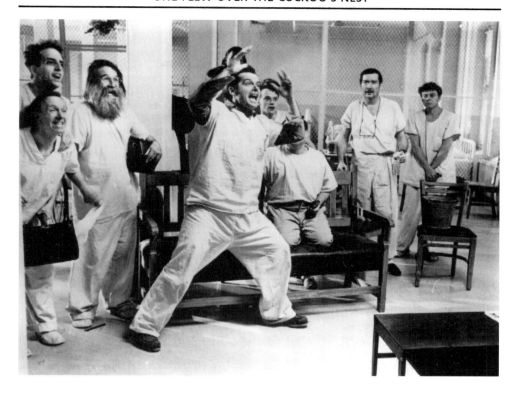

provide entertainment for the other inmates – or his mental illness manifesting itself, does he genuinely "see" the game?

After another meeting with Dr Brooks where McMurphy expresses his intense dislike of Nurse Ratched who he accuses of "Not playing the rules...", in the next sequence, McMurphy, enlisting the help of Chief, scales the perimeter fence of the hospital and steals the bus filled with his fellow patients. After picking up his female "friend" Candy (a prostitute), McMurphy takes the group on a fishing trip after stealing a boat and convincing the owner of the harbour, that he and his associates are all doctors at the institution, rather than patients. Teaching the other inmates the joys of fishing and leaving Cheswick in charge of the navigation, McMurphy takes Candy below deck for sex. Curious, the rest of the inmates soon search for him and a half-dressed McMurphy returns to upper deck and (again ambiguously) helps the group to catch a fish. The boat later arrives back at the harbour triumphant with a genuine catch of fish to boast, and to the awaiting attentions of the hospital staff and assorted police at the quayside.

The film once again returns to Dr Brooks, involved with a meeting of fellow psychiatrists discussing whether McMurphy's mental disorders are real or feigned before the film switches to the basketball court where McMurphy,

aided by the Chief and other inmates, proves victorious in a basketball game against staff orderlies. Segueing into a group discussion, McMurphy angrily berates the other inmates for not telling him that he is (unlike prison) ineligible for parole at a certain date. Some of the inmates reveal they are at the hospital only on a voluntary basis and soon the discussion turns violent as Chesney – by now having soaked up much of McMurphy's machismo – (childishly) scolds Nurse Ratched for her "childish" rules. In the ensuing chaos McMurphy smashes the glass to Nurse Ratched's office to provide Chesney with his otherwise heavily rationed cache of cigarettes and soon a full scale fight breaks out involving mostly McMurphy and, latterly, Chief who aids his friend after McMurphy is set upon by some of the hospital's male orderlies.

Chesney, Chief and McMurphy find themselves waiting in a corridor for electro shock treatment. Chesney, reduced to hysteria is taken into the room first; leaving Chief and McMurphy alone. It transpires that Chief is neither deaf nor dumb, but has simply been faking it. McMurphy is delighted and they discuss escaping from the hospital, but his rapture is broken when his turn arrives for the shock treatment and in one of the film's more harrowing scenes, he undergoes the treatment in its gruelling, barbaric entirety.

Returning to the ward during group therapy at a later date, McMurphy initially pretends to have been lobotomised, much to his fellow

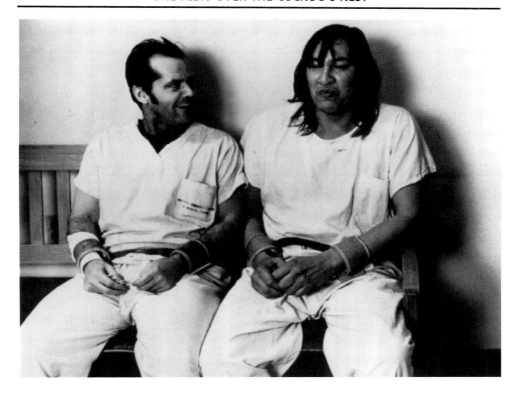

inmates' horror but after a wink to the Chief, he reveals himself in his usual flamboyant glory and the discussion continues without incident.

Yet later that night, McMurphy, after bribing the night porter Turkel (Scatman Crothers, years later to join Nicholson for Kubrick's **The Shining**), succeeds in gaining entry for Candy, another female friend and considerable amounts of alcohol into the ward, and a full-blown party ensues. McMurphy, realising the feelings Billy has for Candy turns sexual liberator for the youth and allows Candy to spend a night with him. Though McMurphy plans to escape, he falls asleep to be awakened next morning by the male orderlies and the arrival of Nurse Ratched. With the ward now partly destroyed by the previous night's revelries, Nurse Ratched orders a count of the inmates and realising that Billy is missing, initiates a search. Billy is found in bed with Candy and is reunited with the inmates to applause and cheering. After berating Billy (and it is noticeable that since his encounter with Candy his masculinity has increased and his stuttering noticeably reduced), Nurse Ratched sends him to a room alone where Billy commits suicide. McMurphy, violently enraged, attempts to strangle Nurse Ratched before being overwhelmed by the orderlies as the tension and hatred which has built up between the two finally explodes in cathartic fury.

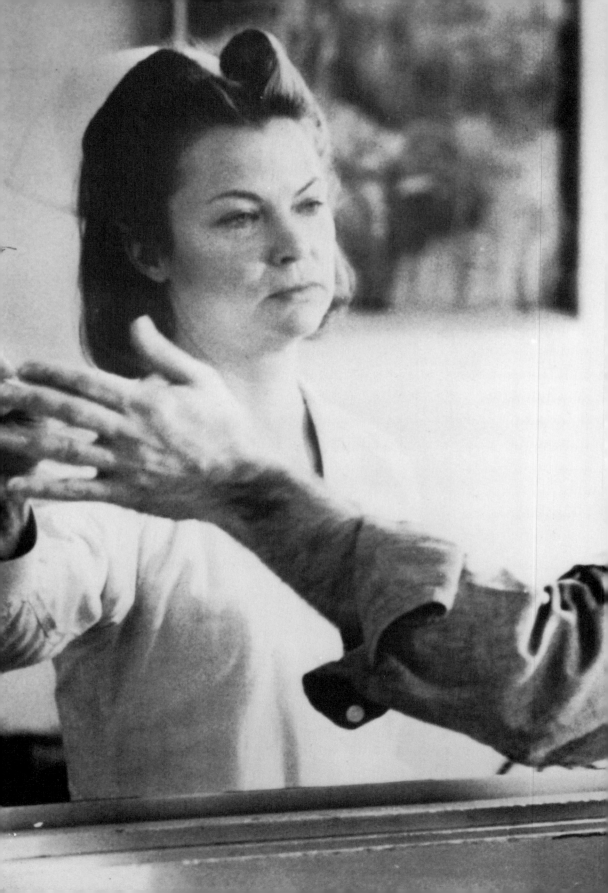

Time has passed and the narrative returns to the ward where, once again, an epitome of structured calm prevails similar to the opening scenes. The inmates are throwing rumours amongst themselves as to the fate of McMurphy, but it is the Chief who late one night sees the figure of McMurphy returning to the ward and being put to bed by two orderlies. Chief greets McMurphy with the news that he feels ready to escape, before noticing that McMurphy has genuinely had a frontal lobotomy and is thus permanently mentally incapacitated. The Chief suffocates McMurphy with a pillow (akin to a mercy killing) and, echoing McMurphy's attempt to smash his way out of the hospital, succeeds in using the heavy shower block as his getaway tool and breaks out. The film ends with Chief running off into the distance, cheered on by the recently awoken inmates.

## THREE

Filming in Oregon would take eleven weeks and Nicholson arranged accommodation for himself and Anjelica Huston, his girlfriend. Huston soon realised her mistake as Nicholson, who became increasingly emotionally involved in his character, proved increasingly impossible to live with. Before flying back to Los Angeles early, producer Michael Douglas apologised to her: "If it's any consolation, this films going to be a smash. I've never been more impressed with any actor in my life". The filming also proved unpleasant for many of the cast and crew and they resorted to hanging around on street corners when not shooting, in attempts to score marijuana off the local populace. This proved embarrassing for the film, so one individual was sent to make a bulk purchase which was then broken down into smaller packages by one of the production assistants and sold at street prices to the actors and crew.

Said Nicholson "Usually I don't have much trouble slipping in and out of a film role, but in Oregon I didn't go home from a movie studio, I went home from a mental institution and there's a certain amount of character left in you that you can't get rid of, you are in a mental ward and that's it. It became harder and harder to create a separation from reality and make believe because some of the people in there look and talk so normal. You would never know they were murderers."

Yet, considering the difficult location and the strong subject matter it is an extraordinary performance from Nicholson, arguably the finest of his career. Balancing the myriad complexities of his character's often polarised ambiguities, Nicholson is at once wholly believable as the flawed, subversive, inspirational but ultimately doomed anti-hero, rallying against the establishment, here symbolised by the omnipotent Nurse Ratchet.

Yet McMurphy is part victor, part victim and part liberator. Most of his fellow patients are (while partly mentally ill), also weak. Most have

voluntarily committed themselves and until McMurphy's arrival, have been content to simply submit to Nurse Ratched's delusions of grandeur. Sexual politics manifests itself early on. McMurphy soon berates his fellow patients for their femininity, for sitting around and talking about their problems at the behest of Nurse Ratched's indulgences. McMurphy entertains more masculine notions (and is especially keen to become both mentor and sexual liberator for Billy Bibbit), and after his arrival and his consequent feeding of a steady dose of poker, fishing, baseball and easy young women to his fellow inmates, the men rapidly become more aggressively masculine and Nurse Ratched, who begins to lose her rein of power, turns to the system itself to find more potent methods of control.

Ostensibly, **Cuckoo's Nest** has remained one of the most prominent Hollywood films to portray psychiatry as a weapon in the considerable and perpetual battle that society uses against its non-conformist members. Arguably the most famous mental institution film (a sub-genre of the prison movie) and certainly the most potent since Anatole Litvak's **The Snake Pit** (1948), the institution in **Cuckoo's Nest** is nevertheless portrayed as explicitly worse than prison. Dr Brooks would later add weight to this argument by berating the producers for certain inaccuracies within the film, though he said "It is a great honour to do a scene with Jack Nicholson, who is an absolute genius in getting across the character of McMurphy, a sociopath of whom there are plenty around. Jack's performance typified them". Moreover, Dr Brooks admits experiencing a number of criticisms from colleagues who felt the film had "...set psychiatry back twenty-five years," but defends both his involvement and the film itself by arguing that the view of the film as a negative portrayal of psychiatry is a narrow one, Kesey rather than writing about mental hospitals in particular was simply writing about institutions in general, and that the film raised society's awareness and increased the number of concerns about institutions.

The film is also a prime example of a left film (a right film finds psychiatry represented by ineffectual psychiatrists addressing the problems that are ultimately resolved by vigilante violence and the hero surviving the oft climactic ending of the film). **Cuckoo's Nest** finds psychiatry a more ominous force however, and the anti-hero McMurphy whilst portrayed as an almost Christ like saviour (and of course dying for his sins) proves, following one violent misdemeanour too many, ultimately no match for the destructive power of the establishment. But the fact that we sympathise with McMurphy come his brutal yet inspirational (to others) defeat is testament largely to Nicholson's vibrant and multi-textual rendering of the character. [Similar examples of left films include **Cool Hand Luke** (1967), **Easy Rider** (1969), **Kid** (1969) and **Bonnie And Clyde** (1967). In America at least, the sixties image of the doomed anti-hero was due in part to the idealistic turmoil that greeted both the Kennedy assassination and the Vietnam War – although Jean-Luc Godard's **Breathless** (1961), a famously influential film for American filmmakers, would offer up the same embryonic character type.]

Structurally, tonally and thematically, **Cuckoo's Nest** is executed with remarkable precision. Neither indulgent in length or with an erroneous and bloated scene in its entire length, Nicholson while taking the lion's share of the critical praise for his cohesive and controversial libertarianism was substantially aided in his performance by the high quality of the performances from the ensemble cast. For while the film offers up a sharp and often unflinching view of institutionalised life (and its filming in a genuine hospital rather than on a sound stage, and the use of eighty-seven inmates from the hospital in peripheral roles added immeasurably to the realism), Nicholson injects a suitable amount of humour into the occasionally sentimentalised proceedings in what would have otherwise have been a grim film indeed. But that **Cuckoo's Nest** suggests that institutions are the last place individuals should go if they want to be "cured" is hardly a unique staple of the genre. The sensational elements used in the film including electro-convulsive therapy, sexual repression tablets and use of the lobotomy can be found in many other films in the genre including **Shock Corridor** (1963), **Shock Treatment** (1964) and **Frances** (1982) amongst others. And like **Frances** (the Jessica Lange starring film biopic of Frances Farmer, golden era Hollywood actress, forced to degrade herself in films and thrust into an institution by her mother after she gives up the profession, only to endure rape, insulin injections and electro-shock treatment), **Cuckoo's Nest** shares similar themes – the less than subtle suggestion that society itself is upside down and that the truly mentally disturbed remain outside the institutions while the few non-conformist, needy but largely charismatic individuals are incarcerated.

Director Milos Forman, despite Kesey's explosive text and Nicholson's verve, was not to be overshadowed however. Considering an enormously difficult project to bring to the screen, esteemed film biographer David Thompson sums up, "...Forman deserves great credit for the sudden but controlled movements from hilarity to tragedy. The metaphor of the insane institution works in terms of challenging entertainment largely because of Forman's very balanced awareness that oddity, madness and acting are overlapping conditions."

Both a critical and commercial smash, **One Flew Over The Cuckoo's Nest** would garner nine Oscar nominations and would walk away with five during the 1976 ceremony in what was, in retrospect, a golden year for Hollywood movies. Nicholson was dramatically vindicated for his performance by winning Best Actor (elbowing out Walter Matthau for **The Sunshine Boys** and Al Pacino for **Dog Day Afternoon**), Louise Fletcher would win in the Best Actress category for her terrifying and effortlessly heartless performance and the film would take Best Adapted Screenplay. Equally significant were the results in the two top awards, Best Film and Best Director. **Cuckoo's Nest** would win Best Film beating four other extraordinary films that year (**Jaws**, **Barry Lyndon**, **Dog Day Afternoon** and **Nashville**), while Milos Forman would win the Best director category in competition with four critically lauded directors: Federico Fellini (**Amarcord**), Stanley Kubrick (**Barry Lyndon**), Sidney Lumet (**Dog Day Afternoon**) and Robert Altman (**Nashville**).

Both Forman and Nicholson would win more Oscars, notably another Best Director Oscar for Forman's multi-award winning **Amadeus** (1984) and Nicholson in a Best Supporting role for **Terms Of Endearment** (1983) and Best Actor for **As Good As It Gets** (1997), but **One Flew Over The Cuckoo's Nest** represents the arguably unequalled pinnacle in both their careers.

# 'THE SHINING'

Since 1969, Jack Nicholson and legendary director Stanley Kubrick – by then responsible for **Paths Of Glory** (1957), **Spartacus** (1960), **Lolita** (1962), **Dr Strangelove** (1963) and **2001 – A Space Odyssey** (1968) amongst others – had talked about working together. The catalyst was Nicholson himself, who, following years of playing low budget horror films and bikers, finally achieved both popularity and critical praise with his Oscar nominated performance as a drunken liberal lawyer in **Easy Rider**. Ten days after seeing **Easy Rider**, Kubrick, then heavily involved with bringing an ambitious historical epic about Napoleon to the big screen – though telling the British press he was considering British actors David Hemmings or Ian Holm to play Napoleon – soon turned to Nicholson as his final choice. He wrote to Nicholson: "You alone have the quality that cannot be acted as an actor. The director cannot create intelligence within a characterisation within an actor and you have it tremendously. It permeates your work."

His praise for Nicholson would go further as Kubrick was to tell Michael Ciment: "I believe that Jack is one of the best actors in Hollywood, perhaps on a par with the greatest stars of the past like Spencer Tracy and Jimmy Cagney. I should think that he is on almost everyone's first choice for a role that suits him. His work is always interesting, clearly conceived and has the X-factor, magic. Jack is particularly suited for roles which require intelligence. He is an intelligent and literate man and these are almost impossible to act."

Nicholson was flattered but before Kubrick could progress past his initial screenplay, the cinema suddenly found an interest in Napoleon and three films would be released in quick succession. They all proved financial failures however, and the astute Kubrick realised that the chances of funding his big-budget film had become too remote to consider. He moved onto other projects, ended up releasing **A Clockwork Orange** in 1971, and the potential collaboration with Nicholson was put on ice.

By 1978, Nicholson was undergoing a mini personal crisis. His stunning Oscar-winning performance in Milos Forman's **One Flew Over The Cuckoo's Nest** was already three years distant and his 1977 directorial debut **Goin' South**, a comedy Western in which he starred as Henry Moon, an inept, unkempt bank robber (with a drugged out John Belushi in cameo mode), received both a savage critical mauling and minimal box office. Nicholson's way over the top performance (fuelled by barely denied rumours of rampant on-set cocaine consumption) would create the lion's share of the criticism. With the recent break-up in his long time and highly tumultuous relationship to actress Angelica Huston, the current revelations of his dysfunctional childhood – having been brought up to believe his grandmother

was his mother and his true mother his elder sister – the Roman Polanski affair (the drugging, rape and sodomy of an underage girl at Nicholson's mansion) – and Nicholson's then well-documented use of narcotics, the actor was understandably in an agitated mental state.

Then he received a call from Kubrick. Following **A Clockwork Orange**, Kubrick's most recent film – the languidly paced though extraordinarily beautiful historical drama **Barry Lyndon** – had been released in 1974 to solid European business and Oscar nominations, though little financial success Stateside. Since then Kubrick had been flirting with ideas for his next feature. During this lengthy brainstorming, Warner Bros Executive John Calley who'd read Stephen King's novel *The Shining*, sent a copy to Kubrick, knowing his long-standing interest in the paranormal. King himself had become a publishing superstar. When *The Shining* was released, King was thirty-two years old and had sold 22 million copies of six novels including *Carrie* and *Salem's Lot*. Kubrick had never read a King novel before Calley sent him the book (though he had seen and reportedly enjoyed Brian de Palma's film of *Carrie*), but was immediately fascinated with the structural framework of the text.

While reading the story for the first time, Kubrick cast the film with Nicholson his clear choice for Jack Torrance and Shelley Duvall, who Kubrick considered a "wonderful actress" his vision of Torrance's tormented wife Wendy. Said Nicholson: "I had just finished a summer's work on a script I was

hoping to direct [**Goin' South**] when Stanley called out of the blue and asked if I would be interested in working with him on his next movie. I hadn't read the book but it wouldn't have mattered. I would have done whatever Stanley wanted. He sent me a copy of the book. I have been quoted as saying that I must be 75 percent of every character that I play, but the truth is that I look first for something that holds my attention in the story and then for the overview of a great director. It's an old acting cliché, but you can only be as good as you're willing to be bad. *The Shining* is a wonderful story. I think this movie will be very very good."

*The Shining* was King's longest and most ambitious book to that date. Set in a snowbound Colorado hotel called The Overlook (and built on an ancient Indian burial ground), the book charted the psychological and idealistic deterioration of the winter caretaker Jack Torrance. Torrance was a dour ex-teacher with literary ambitions and a history of alcohol abuse and domestic violence (though the book focused on, and was seen through the eyes of six year old son Danny). Torrance takes the job in the hope it would release him from writer's block to finish a novel. However once he, his wife Wendy and young Danny are alone, the spirits which haunt the hotel (ghosts from atrocities in American history) begin to affect him as they did the previous caretaker, who killed his family with an axe.

King's most inventive creation in the book is a topiary garden, the creatures of which, sculpted from living shrubs, metamorphose as the hotel

becomes snowbound. Wendy and Danny are ultimately saved by the hotel's chef Halloram (played in the film by Scatman Crothers, who appeared alongside Nicholson in both **The King Of Marvin Gardens** and **One Flew Over The Cuckoo's Nest**) who battles through he snow to rescue them, having recognised in Danny the same pre-cognitive and telepathic ability which he possesses and which his Grandmother used to call "shining".

Kubrick, however, while writing the screenplay and rejecting collaboration with King (though he was to use him as a springboard for ideas), was soon to see the book in a wholly different light. Though he was interested in the book's central protagonist Danny, he ultimately decided the story was about Jack, and everything else, including the supernatural elements was peripheral[1].

The deal struck, Nicholson took $1.25 million plus a percentage of the gross and the producers provided him with a London house for £850 a week – which in 1978 was substantial enough to provide him with a four bedroom, four bathroom, four reception room mini-mansion complete with covered garden on an exclusive Chelsea embankment, and a Daimler with a driver named George on 24-hour call outside the front door.

Shooting began early 1978 and Kubrick true to form, released extremely little information about his project to the press, or to the management of Warner Bros and the EMI-Elstree Studio's where the film was being shot. A spokesman told *Variety*: "As befitting of any hotel, Mr Kubrick has just hung up the 'Do Not Disturb' sign". Inside, Kubrick would be using four of Elstree's nine stages.

Kubrick's legendary perfectionism and need to do multiple takes for every scene, would soon begin to take its toll on both the cast and crew. The 69-year-old Scatman Crothers was one of the first to feel the strain. One particular shot of the scene in the kitchen between Danny and Halloram discussing the shining ran at 148 takes. The single shot ran for seven minutes and Kubrick printed every single take. Later Kubrick was to film upwards of forty takes of the scene where Jack Torrance attacks Halloram with an axe. After he had axed the tired actor for the fortieth time, Nicholson asked Kubrick not to continue much longer. The director as usual, was more focused on the film than aware of the needs of his cast, and though Nicholson had obvious reverence for Kubrick's vision and willingly submitted to the demands of his perfectionism, he felt compelled to intervene on Crothers' behalf.

Later in the shoot, Nicholson's scene with Kubrick veteran Joe Turkel playing Lloyd, the ghostly bartender was shot some 36 times. Said Kubrick: "Jack's performance here is incredibly intricate, with sudden changes of thought and mood – all grace notes. It's a very difficult scene to do because the emotional flow is so mercurial. It demands knife-edge changes of direction and a tremendous concentration to keep things sharp and economical. In this particular scene Jack produced his best takes near the highest number."

Director John Boorman, writing in *The Emerald Forest Diary* said: "Kubrick likes to do many takes. Jack Nicholson told me that on **The Shining**, Stanley sometimes did seventy or eighty takes on a set-up. When I saw the film I could see what Kubrick had been up to He was trying to get performances that came out of extremity, exhaustion."

And Nicholson, no stranger to playing pathological characters (not least Randle P McMurphy in **Cuckoo's Nest**) was attracted to Jack Torrance's psychosis. "The book had that intimation to begin with and I just blew it up. It's a demanding, highly difficult performance that's sort of balletic. If you ask the average person to walk down a thirty-yard hallway, they'd start fidgeting after the first ten yards, but an actor has to fill the space. He has to find someplace where the style merges with the reality of the piece, some kind of symbolic design."

As Kubrick had done of his previous films, he continued to re-write the script of **The Shining** as the film slowly progressed through filming, to the extent that Nicholson soon gave up on his original copy and used the daily revisions as his working script. Every time he received new pages, Nicholson would draw a line under his character's name every time it had appeared. He had seen horror legend Boris Karloff use this method when Nicholson had appeared with him on two films directed by Roger Corman, **The Raven** (1962) and **The Terror** (1962), and had done it ever since.

On set Nicholson always appeared in character. He knew the part of Jack Torrance was extremely physical so he often pumped up his adrenaline into a frenzy by jumping up and down and shouting loudly as he prepared for a take. His committed passion for the film and his own intellect would also bring about the most memorable and quoted verbal utterance in the film when Torrance hacks his way through a door with an axe, while his wife Wendy cowers in a corner. When the hole is big enough for his face to squeeze through he shouts "Hereeeee's Johnny", an improvised line neither in the book or the screenplay. When Nicholson suggested it, Kubrick did not understand what it meant (having lived in England since the end of the **Spartacus** shoot in 1961) and was unfamiliar with the introduction to the Johnny Carson show on US television.

Further insights into the film making process were to come from

Kubrick's youngest daughter Vivian, eighteen years old and with aspirations to get into the movies. She was, in a rare breach of her father's customary strict security, allowed to make a video documentary of the film shoot, which later aired on the BBC[2]. Nicholson was to tell the documentary crew: "When I come up against a director that has a concept that maybe I don't agree with, maybe I just hadn't thought about it or whatever, I'd be more prone to go with them than my own because I want to be out of control as an actor. I want them to have the control – otherwise it's going to become predictably my work and that's not fun."

But it was to be Nicholson's manic performance that was to drive the story mercilessly back to the daily paranoia and social dysfunction of the actor's own life. Gordon Stainforth, one of **The Shining**'s editors offered this useful anecdote: "That long tracking shot where Jack Nicholson pursued Shelley Duvall up the staircase while she's waving a baseball at him was taken fifty or sixty times. Typically, Nicholson's first take would be absolutely brilliant. Then the thing would start to get stale after about ten takes. Then you could see he's almost marking time so he doesn't get exhausted. Then he's going right over the top. The impression I got is that Stanley tended to go for the most eccentric and rather over the top ones. There were plenty of times when Stanley and I were viewing the stuff where my private choice of the best performance – or sometimes he would ask me – wasn't in, while the more eccentric was."

And Nicholson was feeling the strain. Intense and lengthy daylong shoots caused Nicholson to say of Kubrick during filming: "I complained that he was the only director to light the sets with no stand-ins. We had to be there even to be lit. Just because you're a perfectionist doesn't mean you're perfect." He told Janet Huck: "Kubrick's demanding. He'll do a scene fifty times and you have to be good to do that. There are so many ways to walk into a room, order breakfast or be frightened to death in a closet. Stanley's approach is, how can we do it better than it's ever been done before? It's a big challenge. A lot of actors give him what he wants. If you don't, he'll beat it out of you... with a velvet glove of course."

Though the film began shooting in May 1978, such was Kubrick's demands for technical excellence, that the film would not wrap filming until April 1979. Elstree Studios, not having planned to allow Kubrick that amount of time, were forced to juggle other films in the schedule including Dino De Laurentiis's production of **Flash Gordon** (1980) and George Lucas's production of **The Empire Strikes Back** (1980), the second instalment of the original **Star Wars** trilogy.

Visually, **The Shining** is an often extraordinary and groundbreaking film, not least in terms of the technical aspects. With the liberal use of Garrett Brown's dramatic new invention the Steadicam, which aids some of the most arresting images in the film (young Danny's lengthy tricycle ride round the complex, the camera following him just eighteen inches from the ground, perhaps the most obvious example of virtuoso camerawork), the vast and ultra-realistic looking hotel, bathed in naturalistic light (though the entire hotel was painstakingly created and lit under the supervision of John Alcott at Elstree), and the beautiful helicopter tracking shots taken in the Glacier National park in Montana that make up the opening sequence of the film (and out-takes of these would famously turn up at the denouement of Ridley Scott's futuristic and *noir*-esque **Bladerunner**), it remains a visually and technically dazzling film.

Of Nicholson's performance itself, David Thomson, writer of the excellent *A Biographical Dictionary Of Film* writes: "**The Shining** was one of his great films – the wicked, naughty boy, the thwarted genius, the monster of his own loneliness. No one else could have been so daring and yet so delicate."

It is an appraisal that whilst largely valid, is perhaps over adulatory. Nicholson certainly offers up an intensely manic performance (that out-energises even his McMurphy in **One Flew Over The Cuckoo's Nest**), and

his ability to both mesmerize the eye and fill the frame has rarely been as pronounced in any other film in his considerable canon. Yet as Kubrick was to tell Michael Ciment: "In **The Shining** you believe he's a writer, failed or otherwise." This point is certainly valid; Nicholson of course had, prior to filming, written the screenplay to **Goin' South** as well as several scripts in the '60s, and consequently was easily able to absorb and convincingly portray the nuances of a frustrated scribe.

Nicholson was to tell Ron Rosenbaum: "That's the one scene in the movie I wrote myself. That scene at the typewriter – that's what I was like when I got my divorce. I was under the pressure of being a family man with a daughter and one day I accepted a job to act in a movie in the daytime and I was writing a movie at night and I'm back in my little corner and my beloved wife Sandra, walked in on what was unbeknownst to her, this maniac – and I told Stanley about it and we wrote it into the scene. I remember being at my desk and telling her, 'Even if you don't hear me typing it doesn't mean I'm not writing. This is writing.'" Rosenbaum, who wrote a feature on Nicholson for the *New York Times Magazine*, would go further and call the film "the first horror movie about writer's block".

Yet the film on its release, though keenly anticipated by the legions of Stephen King fans and Kubrick devotees, proved ultimately a less than successful critical endeavour. While suffused with an eerie atmosphere, some arresting images of violence, and often resonant with moral and mental decay, the film largely fails to fully engage the emotional responses; something King's ironic text achieved far more successfully. Arguably the film remains too cold and soulless to absolutely captivate, the structural narrative too formatted, and thus the film suffers in its deliberate detachment; leading to character performances that whilst infused with hyper-realism, fail to elicit sympathy throughout.

Biographer David Thomson disagrees. "**The Shining** for me, is Kubrick's one great film, so rich and comic that it offsets his several large failures. The elements of the horror story have been turned into a study of isolation, space and the susceptible imagination of the man who lacks the skills to be a writer. **The Shining** is about intuitive intimations, good or bad, and it has an intriguingly detached view of its story's apparent moral situation. Perhaps Jack Torrance is a monster, a dad run amok, perhaps family is the suffocation that anyone should dread. The film is very funny (especially as Nicholson goes over his edge), serenely frightening and endlessly interesting. For the Overlook Hotel is not just a great set, but a museum of movies, waiting for ghostly inhabitants."

Perhaps tellingly, **The Shining** would end up as the first Kubrick film in 23 years not to garner any Oscar nominations (not since **Paths of Glory**). Stephen King was to pronounce himself less than satisfied with the film on its release and though the film proved a box office success for Warner Bros and one of Kubrick's most commercially successful films (its opening weekend box office proved bigger than either **The Exorcist** or **Superman**), critically it would be one of Kubrick's least praised films.

# NOTES

1.  Kubrick considered including King's animal-shaped hedges that came to life and could morph, but the special effects options did not satisfy his strict specifications for believability and he knew the effects would put an impossible strain on the $13 million budget. Instead he decided to create a huge maze replete with complex arrangements of alleys and angles.

2.  Vivian had no formal training but Kubrick, true to his belief that the best way to learn film-making was to make a film, gave her an Aaton 16mm camera and told her film as much as she liked, with the condition that he be allowed approval of the final cut. At his urging, certain scenes showing him in a less than flattering light were later removed. Scenes of Nicholson dropping his trousers, some of the cast taking reviving lines of cocaine and Kubrick famously losing his temper with actress Duvall would remain.

# "WE HAD A DEAL": FAUSTIAN BARGAINS IN 'THE WITCHES OF EASTWICK'

According to legend, the devil was once a star. Christian tradition casts him as Lucifer ("lightbearer" in Latin and a name for the planet Venus) – the angelic "son of the morning" who, through perverse pride, became God's enemy only to be cast, "headlong flaming", into the pit of Hell.[1] A powerful presence in Western imagination since at least the middle ages, the devil is also a scene stealer. As all literature students know, John Milton's *Paradise Lost* (source of the epithet "headlong flaming") hands Lucifer all the best lines and scenes, a situation definitely not intended by Milton, who was the most upright and orthodox of Puritans. According to William Blake, the figure of Lucifer exerted such imaginative force that Milton was drawn to it against conscious intention:

*The reason Milton wrote in fetters when he wrote of angels & God, and at liberty when of devils & hell, is because he was a true poet and of the devil's party without knowing it.*[2]

In George Miller's 1987 film **The Witches Of Eastwick** (loosely based on John Updike's novel), the devil is portrayed by that biggest of stars, Jack Nicholson. A wry allegory about feminism and patriarchal anxiety, the film, like its devil, eschews Milton's Gothic gravity in favour of a languid cheekiness. *This* devil is a ponytailed hipster, filthy rich art collector and silver-tongued seducer of women. Middle-aged and a bit paunchy, he nonetheless has more than enough charm to get by. In other words, Nicholson's Daryl Van Horne is nothing so much as a caricature of Jack Nicholson himself.

Indeed, **Witches...** can be seen as one of a series of mid-80s films in which Nicholson riffs self-consciously on aspects of his own superstar persona. Whereas his early, breakthrough performances (**Carnal Knowledge, Five Easy Pieces**) were subtle and character-driven, these later efforts – Charlie in **Prizzi's Honor**, Mark in **Heartburn**, Van Horne in **Witches...**, the Joker in **Batman** – are broad and cartoonish, with the feel of static images. What depth they have derives from (and depends on) the audience's familiarity with the great star's life and work and the implied comparison between this biographical information and the on-screen diegesis. In **Prizzi's Honor**, for example, Nicholson brings little more to the part of Charlie Partanna than tics, tricks and crude stereotyping. The real interest lies in the fact that it's *Jack*, mugging through a mobbed-up soap opera opposite his real-life ex-paramour, the formidable Anjelica Huston. This is to say that Nicholson's stardom overshadows the performance, a situation that may be inescapable for – or essential to being – a screen icon. Given Nicholson's early work though, it's tempting to call it a fall from grace.

In **The Witches Of Eastwick**, Nicholson offers one of these cartoonish performances, one whose subtext is the Faustian nature of superstardom. Few actors ever succeed in making a decent living, let alone in becoming famous. Those who become stars must feel a bit like the pale scholar who traded his soul for worldly power and glamour. And Jack Nicholson is, arguably, the biggest Hollywood star of the late twentieth century. As David Thomson recounts, "When it was time for the presentation of best picture at the 1993 Oscars, Billy Crystal had only to say 'Jack', and everyone knew who was coming".[3] Though his character in **Witches...** is called Daryl Van Horne, Nicholson is really playing "Jack", that horny devil, in what may be an attempt at exorcism.

The theme of **Witches...** is the rise of feminism in relation to a particular kind of masculinity; specifically, the cultural archetype that feminist philosopher Mary Daly calls the "Dionysian male".[4] Here too, Nicholson's stardom is key, for his most popular characterizations – George Hanson in **Easy Rider**, Bobby Dupea in **Five Easy Pieces**, McMurphy in **One Flew Over The Cuckoo's Nest** – can be seen as varying aspects of this archetype. This model of masculinity came to contemporary prominence with the counterculture of the 1960s and '70s, the period of Nicholson's own ascendancy, and Nicholson's image is inextricably bound up with it. However, in the neo-conservative 1980s, this figure, like the counterculture itself, came to be viewed by many as a problematic, even poisonous, presence on the cultural scene. Indeed, for feminists, it began to look like the old patriarchy in only slightly more appealing garb. In **The Witches Of Eastwick**, Nicholson attempts to give this devil his due.

## THE DEAL

In the sleepy New England village of Eastwick, three single women spend their days dealing with jobs that are dreary, prospects that are dim and men who are dull and/or predatory. The ranks of the latter include weasely ex-husbands, dispirited do-gooders and butt-patting bosses pitching quid pro quos. Each Thursday evening the three get together at one or another's house for drinks, dinner and sisterly socializing.

The three women are: Jane Spofford (Susan Sarandon), a mousy schoolmarm who teaches band to tuneless kids while enduring the advances of her married principal; Sukie Ridgemont (Michelle Pfeiffer), a waiflike reporter for the local newspaper and divorced mother of four; and Alexandra Medford (Cher), an assertive, widowed sculptress who specializes in goddess figurines resembling the Venus of Willendorf. With skills in the musical, linguistic and plastic arts respectively, they cover the aesthetic waterfront like three suburban graces. They also evoke, in ironic form, the triple goddess of neo-pagan myth: Jane is an old maid(en), Sukie an earth mother, and Alexandra, with her neolithic goddesses and merry widow status, a sort of crone.

Such primal qualities bespeak female power – a power that is magnified among women who share each other's company and who are unattached to men. Add to the mix strong drink, resentment and smouldering desire, and you have a potent brew, one that will enable the three to summon the man of their dreams. Over margaritas one Thursday they shift from complaining to fantasizing. Their ideal man should be nice, talkative and a little brainy. He should be dark and mysterious, like a romantic prince under a curse. He must be handsome, of course, but not too much so, sporting nice eyes, nice ass and a penis that's... well, just right, don't you know.

They're just kidding around of course, but the next morning brings news that the old Lenox mansion – scene of witch burnings centuries before – has been purchased by a mysterious stranger from New York. Reportedly wifeless, he is searching for the right space in which to house his grand piano collection. Enter Nicholson as Daryl van Horne. Each woman will first encounter him by way of her specialty: Sukie through the paper's gossip column; Alex through the sale of all her goddess figurines; and Jane through a string recital.

It is at the recital that we first glimpse Van Horne – eyes closed, jaw slack, head upside down. Seated in the back row, he snoozes through the performance, emitting a bestial racket more like snorting than snoring. The camera shot emphasizes Nicholson's pointed chin and pronounced widow's peak. Framed this way, the star's visage resembles the goat's-head-in-inverted-pentagram symbol familiar to satanic lore. It's a sort of anti-glamour shot and sets up a perversely grand entrance: at the last chord, Van Horne tips over backward, pratfalls to the floor and then shakes himself awake in time to offer an ebullient one-man standing ovation. As we will throughout the film, we sense Nicholson winking – poking us in the ribs as if to say, "Do you *believe* this guy?".

In short order Van Horne deepens his acquaintance with each of the three women. First to venture in the direction of the Lenox mansion, Alex is smoothly intercepted by its owner and treated to a lavish luncheon on the lawn of the estate. Afterwards Van Horne takes her on a tour of the mansion that ends in the boudoir, where he dons a smoking jacket. Next he is on all fours, on the bed – which "once belonged to the Borgias" – nuzzling and writhing like a sultan in heat. "I always like a little pussy after lunch," he

explains, and then, with raunchy aplomb: "Would you prefer to be on the bottom or the top?". It is one of the more hilarious comic turns in Nicholson's repertoire. Both disgusted and amused, Alex tells him off but good. Nonetheless she finds fascinating the sort of man who would do such a thing. "Who *are* you?," she asks, to which Van Horne replies, "Just your average horny little devil," and she soon accepts his offer.

Over lunch, Van Horne discourses volubly on topics dear to Alex's heart, a ploy he will use with each of the women. In Alex's case, it's the oppressiveness of marriage and the general vileness of men. Later, with Jane, the hook will be musical performance (Van Horne plays violin in the heavy metal Romantic mode) and the question of technique (her strong point) versus "passion" (her weak point, until this transforming encounter). Still later, with Sukie, the ostensible topic will be child-bearing, child-rearing and the essential "naturalness" of Woman.

Of course in each case the real topic is Van Horne himself – the one man who's not like the others, who *really* understands. In the midst of a rehearsal with Jane he declaims, "Men are such cocksuckers, aren't they? Their dicks get limp when confronted by a woman of obvious power and

what do they do about it? Call them witches, burn them, torture them until every woman is afraid; afraid of herself, afraid of men and all for what? [Pause] "Fear of losing their hard-on. Now. Let's play some music."

Subject to such attentions the women blossom, psychically and physically, into – well – *stars*, and are soon ensconced at the mansion, where they languish sybaritically when they're not playing psychokinetic tennis. With Van Horne as tutor, they learn to focus and refine their power, first to move inanimate objects, then to make themselves fly; a development that makes possible several cinematic set pieces. The most striking of these is a music video-like sequence set in Daryl's ballroom. Floating like Baroque cherubs, the characters and their children cavort amid hundreds of balloons, accompanied by an aria from Puccini's *Turandot*.

Such flamboyant displays make Van Horne the focus of local gossip. Arousing curiosity in most, he evokes fear and suspicion in the upstanding, snobbish Felicia Alden (Veronica Cartwright), owner of the local newspaper and wife of Sukie's boss, Clyde (Richard Jenkins). Felicia senses evil afoot. Soon, following a mysterious fall, she's diagnosed with a bone marrow disorder that affects her brain. As a result she becomes more and more "hysterical" and "paranoid", obsessed with the perfidy of Van Horne and the three women. She has episodes, seizures, visions. "I've got nothing against a good fuck," she tells her husband, "but there's danger here."

With such material, Cartwright almost steals the film: her Felicia stares, writhes and spews fluid like a society matron possessed. Her utterances, at first eloquent and outraged, gradually become pure Tourette's: overcome in church by a vision of the mansion, she screams, "Whores! Dildoes! Anal intercourse!" and has to be dragged away by the hangdog Clyde. "I open my mouth," she says early on, "and the strangest things come out." Her antics rival those of Nicholson himself, which is fitting, for her character is both his foil and his victim.

Felicia's visions and outbursts are read as madness by the townfolk, making her a Cassandra figure. This is to say that she's a sort of witch as well, albeit one who's on the side of family values and snowy egrets (a local species displaced by Van Horne's real estate developments). Her final insight: he intends to *propagate!* ("They'll bear him sons. He'll take their loving and continue to destroy the earth with it.") Thanks to Felicia's influence, the newspaper runs a sensational exposé on the goings-on at the mansion. Local opinion begins to turn: the women are called sluts and hounded from public places. Sukie is fired from her job. This means Felicia must be stopped, of course, and Van Horne manipulates the women into doing so. At the mansion one evening, they lounge in a Roman bath, nibbling cherries and discussing Felicia's meddling. The women don't realize it, but their power is at work in the form of imitative magic. Back in town, Felicia endures her most severe oral episode, with cherries – hundreds of them – as the main course. (If they gave Oscars for projectile vomiting, this performance would be a contender.) Felicia dies soon afterward, and the women are horrified. ("Last night – those words... They make things happen!") They resolutely break off relations with Van Horne, against his protests. But then Jane turns up pregnant.

Arriving at the mansion to announce her condition, Jane finds Van Horne in his TV room, lounging before a wall-size bank of screens. He's reverted to a drooling, demonic state, replaying videos in which the women discuss their deepest fears. It's pretty clear what he intends to do with this information. Jane escapes unnoticed, but meanwhile Sukie falls gravely ill.

Alex goes to reason with Van Horne ("You can't use your power to hurt people"). She finds him acting like a resentful, neglected housewife, ironing in his bathrobe and watching *Wheel Of Fortune*. "We had a *deal!*" he bellows. Van Horne begs for his "family" to be reunited. After scolding him briefly, Alex agrees.

It's all a ruse, though. Trailing clouds of glamour like before, the women return but soon send Van Horne out for food to satisfy Jane's pregnant cravings. While he's gone they fashion, from his effects, a voodoo doll which they will use to control him. "We're not trying to hurt him," Alex admonishes, "just send him away."

The various magical torments subsequently visited upon Van Horne

make for another comedic romp, culminating in his being blown, literally, into the church where Felicia earlier had her breakdown. Here he delivers a spontaneous sermonette punctuated by the regurgitation of cherries. ("Don't worry," he tells the congregation, "It's a cheap trick. I taught it to'em... I'm having a little domestic problem.") His message: "Do you think God knew what he was doing when he created woman, or was that just another one of his mistakes? Because when *we* make mistakes, they call it evil. But when God makes mistakes, they call it *nature*... I wanna know, because if it's a mistake, then maybe we can find a *cure*..." With its over-the-top energy and leering sarcasm, the speech is classic Jack.

Eventually Van Horne returns to the mansion where a magical battle royal ensues, driven by some cheesy special effects. When the smoke clears, Van Horne has shrunk to homuncular size. He gibbers, twitches and then – pop! – disappears.

Eighteen months later, the mansion is occupied by the women, their children and three newborn baby boys. Fidel, Van Horne's well hung though eunuchoid manservant, has been completely domesticated, serving as babysitter and one-man house band. Blissfully in their element, the women have but one caution: not to think of *him* when they're together. No one, after all, really wants him back.

Cut to the TV room down the hall. On the wall-size bank of screens we see a smiling Van Horne, beckoning to his "boys", who toddle in looking rapt. "This'll be our little secret," he advises. "Now come over here and give daddy a big kiss." Suddenly the women appear, scowling, brandishing the remote control. "Aw ladies, come on," says Van Horne, but the power is literally in their hands and the devil is dispatched with a click.

## THE FINE PRINT

The phenomenon – and mystery – of fatherhood has been a consistent theme in Nicholson's personal life, much discussed in celebrity profiles. Biographies paint Nicholson's family history as convoluted, complicated by out-of-wedlock pregnancies and secret adoptions back in the old country.[5] According to David Thomson, a rumour once circulated that Nicholson was the son of a former CEO of American International Pictures; the truth, on the other hand, relates him to "a small-town alcoholic of Irish descent."[6]

With their symmetry and suggestion of mystery, such accounts have the flavour of folklore. Conceived in the heart of Hollywood, near the pinnacle of the American system, the amazing Nicholson was to the manor – and the manner – born; except that he appears to have emerged from society's lowest depths. Then again – we're dealing with movie *magic* here, folks – perhaps he came from both places. And then there's Nicholson himself – seducer, lover, serial cohabiter and, finally, father of (among other offspring) a child conceived out of wedlock whom he has been reluctant to acknowledge.

A 1980s *Vanity Fair* cover featured Nicholson in his new role of patriarch by picturing him holding two babies, "purportedly his". The term "role", however, turns out to have been doubly appropriate, for "the small print admitted these babies were models! Actors!"[7]

In addition to evoking Nicholson's personal difficulties with fatherhood, the film's final scenes play on fears that are patriarchal in a larger sense – i.e., male fears of a feminist society in which men are either superfluous or else reduced to the status of inseminating drones. Such an impression of feminist goals has been voiced by Norman Mailer, among others.[8] Sometimes lumped with Mailer as a white male author whose works reproduce misogynistic ideologies, Updike has conceded that a sort of genteel chauvinism imbues much work by male writers of his generation. However, he denies any hint of misogyny in his own fiction: "I am a white male born at a certain time, probably with some of the baggage of men of my age and vocation. But I can't believe I'm misogynist. Rather the contrary... I was enough aware of feminist criticisms that my novels always had these same male, sexist, lusty heroes that I did try to write a book involving women as heroes..."[9]

The book to which Updike refers is, of course, *The Witches Of Eastwick*. But whereas the novel takes the women as its focus, the film privileges the male lead even as it dramatizes his rejection by the women. There is no way around the fact that this is a Jack Nicholson movie, or that he dominates the film. Indeed, the female stars seem to have been chosen partly for the ways in which they adorn the male lead: they balance each other in terms of traditional categories of glamour – one brunette, one redhead, one blonde; and, as if this were some Hollywood harem, each politely awaits her turn with the male star. Admittedly this device sets up the later rejection of Van Horne, but even there he figures as the absent centre around which the women's concerns revolve: "Jane... Stop it! Not when the three of us are together... Do you want him *back*?"

In a contemporaneous talk show appearance, comedienne Sandra Bernhard joked about this situation, asking whether the audience could imagine a Hollywood scenario in which a short, aging, overweight *female* star might figure as an irresistible object of desire, one capable of enchanting male stars of the calibre of Pfeiffer, Sarandon and Cher.[10] It's good to be the king, she suggested, or at least Jack Nicholson.

Such a conservative subtext is perhaps predictable in a film produced entirely by men. The *faux* feminist tease of **Witches...** is reminiscent of more recent media offerings like *Ally McBeal*, an ostensible "chick show" which is scripted entirely by a man (David Kelley, husband of Michelle Pfeiffer) and whose plots are mostly male fantasies dressed up as "women's issues". While such "transvestism" on the part of male writers can be seen as a commendable attempt to engage the Other, social critic Mary Daly suggests it is analogous to white performers playing blackface, a gesture in which whites incorporate the oppressed role "without being incorporated in it".[11]

Daly, a feminist philosopher and self-described "witch", has written of the dangers posed to women by the figure she calls the "Dionysian male".[12] Greek god of wine, ecstasy and what Freud called the unconscious, Dionysus was framed by Nietzsche as the radical opponent to Apollo, god of light, order and reason. According to Nietzsche, the Apollonian principle demanded "maintenance of the boundaries of the individual, *moderation* in the Hellenic sense" and banished excess to the outer darkness.[13] In contrast, Dionysian ecstasy swamped the individual ego with the roaring tide of the life-force. "In the mystical triumphal cry of Dionysus the spell of individuation is broken and the path is opened to the Mothers of Being, to the innermost core of things."[14] In this supremely altered state, ordinary identity and humanity were pushed aside and the individual possessed by daemonic forces that might as easily prove destructive as blissful. According to Nietzsche, Apollonian order was the keystone of Greek civilization; but without occasional experiences of Dionysian transgression and transcendence, the civilized life was not worth living.[15] Moreover, the glories of Greek tragic art are attributable to a brief, shining historical moment when the tension between these two archetypes was in perfect balance.[16] Since then, Nietzsche suggests, Apollonian intellectualism has dominated – and deformed – Western civilization, amid periodic outbreaks of Dionysian enthusiasm and/or hysteria.[17]

Dionysus has a special relation to women and the feminine. Compared to other male Olympians, he represents a feminized masculinity. He is typically depicted as a beautiful, androgynous youth who leads a band of woodland-dwelling women (*bacchantes* or *maenads*) who've been made mad by his power. Euripides' *The Bacchae* portrays him as the lithe, longhaired leader of a female cult decried by city authorities for its (supposed) lascivious sensuality. King Pentheus – a rigid, militaristic study in male hysteria – attempts to suppress the movement and is decapitated by his own mother.[18]

Though there are a number of similarities between the figure of Dionysus and that of Christ[19], the wine god also bears a resemblance to the Christian figure of the devil. In Greco-Roman myth, Pan, horned god of the woodlands, was a votary of Dionysus. In religious history, this figure provided much of the iconography – horns, goatee, cloven hoofs – which came to characterize depictions of Satan. According to medieval witch-hunter's lore, a witch was a woman who made a pact with the devil, exchanging allegiance for magical power, a pact which was celebrated in woodland revels with the horned lord of darkness.[20]

The late twentieth century has seen numerous scholarly re-interpretations of the witch-craze, many of which diagnose medieval European society as pathologically masculinist. From this perspective, witch-hunting looks like institutionalized misogyny and the witch-craze, a women's holocaust. In such a setting, "witch" is the demonizing label for any woman whose behaviour is seen as transgressing patriarchal norms.[21] Indeed, this is the view of Daly herself.

In *Gyn/Ecology*, Daly notes the call, from sixties-period social philosophers like Norman O. Brown and Sam Keen, for a return of the Dionysian spirit. These male intellectuals see the modern West as dehumanized by its worship of Apollonian reason and repression. The cure is a healthy dose of the Dionysian.[22] But, says Daly, Dionysus is only slightly less insidious than Apollo, for he represents the same old patriarchal principle in female-friendly drag:

*"The seduction of women – including feminists – into confusion by Dionysian boundary violation happens under a variety of circumstances. A common element seems to be an invitation to 'freedom'. The feminine Dionysian male*

*guru or therapist invites women to spiritual or sexual liberation, at the cost of loss of Self in male-dictated behaviour. Male propagation of the idea that men, too, are feminine – particularly through feminine behaviour by males – distracts attention from the fact that femininity is a man-made construct, having essentially nothing to do with femaleness. The seductive preachers of androgyny, of 'human liberation', dwell upon this theme of blending. When they put on the mask of Dionysus, the Myth-Masters play the role of Mix-Masters. 'Mixing Up the Victim' is the name of their mime.*"[23]

Women who traffic with such men are making a deal with the devil, Daly suggests. And indeed, this description captures much of Daryl Van Horne, a man who's "not like all the others", who's neither afraid of female power nor desperate to protect his virility. In fact, part of his seducer's armoury is a similar-sounding critique of patriarchal oppression and hypocrisy ("Men are such cocksuckers, aren't they?"). Like the women themselves, he is the victim and enemy of a social order controlled by and for more conventional (i.e., Apollonian, Pentheus-type) males. Or so he claims.

Like the maenads, the women of Eastwick are enchanted by this figure, joining him in unconventional pleasures on the outskirts of town. As in Euripides, this arouses ire and suspicion among city authorities. Interestingly however, the Pentheus figure in **Witches...** is a woman, Felicia Alden. Like Pentheus, she will be struck down for opposing Dionysian power. And as in *The Bacchae*, the maenads will do the dirty work, on the suggestion – and under the influence – of the Dionysian male.

But in a departure from Euripides, the scapegoat in **Witches...** is female and Felicia's death the sacrifice – the *female* sacrifice – necessary to break the spell of the Dionysian male. Following it, the women rescind their pact – "Aw ladies, come on" – and become custodians of their own liberation, or at least holders of the remote control. A serious joke, that; for **Witches...** is a light comedy, with neither the gravity of Euripides nor the urgency of Mary Daly. Though the film follows a superficially feminist scenario, the horny devil is in the details and these tend to affirm, rather than reject, Dionysian maleness.

## THE CATCH

In contemporary Europe and America, the Dionysian male is a creature of the 1960s. Indeed, from rock music raptures to Mansonian helter skelter, the sixties are often glossed as Western civilisation's last great Dionysian spasm. And more than any other major film star, Nicholson embodies key qualities and contradictions associated with sixties cultural rebellion. Biographies of Nicholson paint him as immersed in sex, drugs and an LA milieu best described as rock'n'roll.[24] And then there is his acting work: If Nicholson's breakthrough comes in the quintessential hippie flick **Easy Rider**, then his apotheosis occurs in **One Flew Over The Cuckoo's Nest**, a film based on the work of Ken Kesey, psychedelic godfather of sixties counterculture.[25] Indeed, Nicholson's films of this period offer a gallery of male portraits, nearly all of them variations on the new, problematized – i.e., Dionysian – masculinity that came to prominence in the period of the Kennedy assassination, Haight-Asbury, Vietnam and Kent State.

Of course Nicholson never played a hippie per se, nor even sported long hair. In fact, many of his great roles hark back to earlier eras of cinema and retain hints of a more traditional masculinity. Jake Gittes in **Chinatown** evokes the droll cynicism of Robert Mitchum; and R.P. McMurphy, of **Cuckoo's Nest**, the roustabout charm of Burt Lancaster. But placed in the larger context of Nicholson's work, alongside strange ducks like George Hanson in **Easy Rider**, Bobby Dupea in **Five Easy Pieces** and Jason Staebler in **The King Of Marvin Gardens**, these "classic" male portrayals look like nostalgic quotations. They suggest that Nicholson's is a masculinity *in transition* and his star appeal that of a synthesizer of conflicting cultural trends.

Such "shifty" maleness is itself Dionysian. Though at times incarnating as Euripides' "effeminate stranger", Dionysus is equally likely to appear as a domineering bull-god.[26] Indeed, according to Daly, the masculinity of Dionysus is not so much transformed as disguised. Though many analysts emphasize Dionysus's female-friendly qualities and lack of conventional machismo, Daly underscores his connections to the Olympian establishment. (He is, after all, the son of Zeus and the cousin of Apollo.) She also considers the myths recounting Dionysus's extraordinary life cycle, noting that they depict females as eminently expendable: Conceived from the rape of a goddess, Dionysus is eventually reborn in the womb of a mortal host-mother who will be incinerated for her trouble. The divine fetus survives of course, and is brought to term by Zeus, who creates an artificial womb in his own thigh. Thus, Dionysus is actually "his own father, reborn and self-generated".[27] For Daly, this scenario suggests a patriarchal agenda that would "eliminate women altogether".[28] Dionysus's real function, she argues, is not so much to challenge patriarchy as to preserve it, by giving it a slightly feminized face.

The sense of a masculinity slightly feminized places Nicholson in the lineage of Marlon Brando and James Dean, stars who carved a space in cinema for a new kind of androgynous male outsider. And while Nicholson is less physically beautiful than Brando or Dean and often behaves like a macho ladykiller, he is feminized in other ways. All the characters mentioned above are men who've fallen on the wrong side of (usually male) power. (In fact, that power, as in **Chinatown** and **Five Easy Pieces**, is often literally patriarchal.) Moreover, in their struggle against such power, Nicholson's characters manifest qualities and conditions – irrationality, artistic sensitivity, playfulness, introversion, even the symbolic castration of a mutilated nose – that are conventionally coded as feminine. Indeed, female characters are attracted to their causes for precisely this reason. (Even in the arguably misogynistic **Cuckoo's Nest** there are those goldhearted hookers.) This is not to say they're feminists, these classically Nicholson males, but neither are they conventional patriarchs. Rather, they are versions of the rebellious or wayward son; a fact which (given patriarchal gender codes) makes them mediate figures, much like Dionysus himself.

This same male persona – young, rebellious, feminized – was central to sixties counterculture. The 1980s, however, signalled a cultural shift. Ronald Reagan's presidential campaign demonized the counterculture and his administration rolled back Kennedy-Johnson policy advances, working to dismantle the welfare state. Stranger still, radical feminists like Catherine MacKinnon and Andrea Dworkin formed coalitions with right-wing moralists to fight pornography (a Faustian bargain of perhaps a different stripe). Both the sixties and the Dionysian male seemed to have worn out their cultural welcome.

**Witches...** both reflects and deflects such trends. Ostensibly feminist, the gender contest in **Witches...** is analogous to play fighting among dogs, its function not the transformation but the preservation of the status quo. Combat is simply a safety valve. For the Dionysian male – an embattled, if not endangered species in the revisionist 1980s – the film provides an inoculation. Daryl Van Horne's punishment is like an erotic spanking – a use of pain in the interest, finally, of pleasure, the phallocentric pleasure of seeing him rise to charm and bedevil once more. And, the film asks, what moviegoer would have it otherwise? After all, it's simply *"Jack"*, to quote Billy Crystal – a shorthand indicating something irrepressible and undeniable, like a force of nature.

## ESCAPE CLAUSE

Evoking Nicholson the superstar, this last remark takes us back to the top. If women make Faustian bargains, so too do audiences and actors. Audiences make their deals with commercial media and that brightest of media emanations, the star. Like the Dionysian male, the star – indeed the entire media system – promises to end alienation while actually working to increase it. Fix your gaze, place your dollars, put your faith *here*, says the screen, and find... ultimate *fulfilment*. And now, please, do it again. And again, just once more. In his final incarnation, flickering in the glow of sixteen TV screens, Daryl Van Horne is a lightbearer whose name is legion. If only deliverance could be had with a click.

Consider too the actor and his image. I submit that for Nicholson the actor, the subtext of **Witches...** is the binding nature of celebrity and the danger posed by it, not so much to artistic integrity, as to artistic mutability or mobility. "That's my job," said Nicholson in a 1986 interview, "to be *other* people."[29]

This returns us to the opening quote from Blake, who celebrated Milton's Lucifer not as lord of Evil but as embodiment of Energy – the fiery, creative energy of desire.[30] Milton's God is a figure of icy detachment and immobility, deathly qualities which mainstream religion nonetheless equates with goodness and godliness. Billed as the star of *Paradise Lost*, God is upstaged by a Lucifer who is at least able to change and willing to fall. And for Romantic artists like Blake, the ultimate sin is not pride but stasis – the inability or refusal to change. As Blake might put it, if the artist is to shine then the star has to fall.

By the 1980s, Nicholson's stardom had become his curse. Donning symbolic horns in **The Witches Of Eastwick**, Nicholson was able to put himself – or rather his superstar alter ego "Jack" – *on*, in what seems an attempt at exorcism. It's interesting to note that Nicholson's next major project was **Ironweed** and the role of Francis Phelan, a return to the old character-driven realism. Perhaps, if only for a while, the banishing worked.

# NOTES

1. For the etymology of "Lucifer", see Richard Barrett, *The Old Enemy: Satan And The Combat Myth* (Princeton, NJ: Princeton UP, 1987) 269. For "son of the morning", see Isaiah 14:12; For angelic pride, see Origen, *De Principiis* 1.5.5. For "headlong flaming", see John Milton, *Paradise Lost* I.45.

2. William Blake, "The Marriage Of Heaven and Hell", *Blake: Selected Writings*, ed. Robert F. Gleckner (NY: Meredith, 1967) 73.

3. David Thomson, "Jack Nicholson", *A Biographical Dictionary Of Film*, 3rd ed. (NY: Knopf, 1994) 545.

4. Mary Daly, *Gyn/Ecology: the Metaethics Of Radical Feminism* (Boston: Beacon, 1978) 64-5.

5. Patrick McGilligan, *Jack's Life: A Biography Of Jack Nicholson* 32-7.

6. Thomson 545.

7. Thomson 546.

8. Norman Mailer, interview with Terri Gross, *Fresh Air*, Natl. Public Radio, WFYI, Philadelphia, 1991.

9. John Updike, "*Salon* Interview: As Close As You Can get to the Stars", *Salon*, n.d., 7 June 1999 <www.salonmagazine.com/08/features/ updike2.html>.

10. Sandra Bernhard, interview with David Letterman, *Late Night With David Letterman*, NBC TV, New York, 1987.

11. Daly 67-8.

12. Daly 64-5.

13. Friedrich Nietzsche, *The Birth Of Tragedy*, trans. Shaun Whiteside, ed. Michael Tanner (NY: Penguin, 1993), 26.

14. Nietzsche 76.

15. Nietzsche 22-3.

16. Nietzsche 27.

17. Nietzsche 76.

18. Euripides, *The Bacchae*, trans. Michael Cacoyannis, New York: New American Library, 1982.

19. For similarities between the figures of Dionysus and Christ, consult Euripides, *The Bacchae*. They include the following: each is a divine being who lives as a mortal man; each is murdered, only to be born again; and each is the product of a miraculous birth, with a mortal for a mother and the supreme being for a father. Moreover, the followers of each deity memorialize him by ritualistically consuming food and wine, which they identify with the deity's flesh and blood. Also, the scene in Euripides where Dionysus is interrogated by Pentheus shows striking similarities to New Testament accounts of Jesus's questioning by Pontius Pilate.

20. Barbara G. Walker, "Pan", *The Woman's Encyclopedia Of Myths And Secrets* (San Francisco, 1983) 765-66; see also Jeffrey Burton Russell, *Mephistoles: The Devil In The Modern World* (Ithaca: Cornell UP, 1986) 226.

21. For a survey of the literature on and debates around this topic, see Margot Adler, "The Wiccan Revival", *Drawing Down The Moon: Witches, Druids, Goddess-Worshippers And Other Pagans In America Today* (Boston: Beacon Pr, 1979) 41-93.

22. Daly 64, 66.

23. Daly 68.

24. See McGilligan, *Jack's Life*.

25. Nicholson's countercultural cinema credentials include his work as screenwriter on Roger Corman's psychedelic exploitation flick **The Trip** (1967), starring Peter Fonda and featuring Dennis Hopper in a supporting role. He also co-wrote the screenplay (and briefly appeared in) **Head** (1968), an underrated phantasmagoria ostensibly starring the Monkees and featuring Frank Zappa in a rare cameo. Bob Rafelson, Nicholson's collaborator on films like **Five Easy Pieces**, served as co-writer and director.

26. For accounts of Dionysus as effeminate stranger, see Euripides 21; 25. For accounts of Dionysus as hypermasculine bull-god, see Euripides 33-35; 52.

27. Daly 66.

28. Daly 66.

29. Jack Nicholson, interview with *Sports Illustrated*, qtd. in
McGilligan, *Jack's Life* n.p.

30. The view of Lucifer articulated by Blake was shared by other Romantics like the Shelleys and Lord Byron, a fact which prompted Robert Southey to dub the Shelley-Byron circle "the Satanic school". This view makes Lucifer analogous to the Greek Prometheus, a figure whose rebellion against God is seen not as sinful but as heroic, since God – the Greek Zeus, in this case – is cast as a tyrant and enemy of mankind. The rationale for such a reading is discussed by Shelley in his preface to *Prometheus Unbound*. See also Nietzsche, 49-50.

# WITH A SMILE LIKE YOURS:
# JACK NICHOLSON IN 'BATMAN'

Once upon a time, 1989 to be exact, there was an ex-Disney animator who decided that for his third film as director, he'd make a dark fable based on a famous comic strip. The comic strip was *Batman*, and it had been filmed before – first as a Saturday matinee serial, then for television, in 1966 when it turned (briefly) into one of the top TV shows of the mid-sixties. The original TV show starred Adam West as billionaire Bruce Wayne, who slid down the Batpole and turned into a Batman wearing purple tights and a pointy eared hat. He was accompanied by Burt Ward as his sidekick Robin, who was given to exclamations beginning "Holy..." and ending with a word or phrase particularly germane to whatever situation he and Batman were in at the time.

In its two-year run, the show adopted and popularised "camp" humour and was spun off to the big screen in the format of a two-episodes-stitched-together feature. Unsurprisingly, this original movie version didn't particularly please hardline fans of the original, darker, comic strip[1]. So when Tim Burton announced he'd be following up **Pee-Wee's Big Adventure** (1985) and **Beetle Juice** (1987) with a blockbuster version of **Batman**, fans watched anxiously to see whether or not it would be a retread of the TV show, a faithful adaptation of the comic strip, or something new entirely.

And something new entirely it was. Gone was the TV bat, with his lycra costume, animated *Pow!*'s and *Zok!*'s and straight-faced *I Am The Law* attitude. Gone too, were Robin[2] and the original version of Gotham City, which looked surprisingly like the sort of mid-sixties upscale communities prowled by any number of mid-sixties TV heroes from *Lassie* to *Lt Amos Burke* and back again. In its place rose a dark, gothic nightmare landscape – a city where modern, turret-topped skyscrapers jostled for position with ancient cathedrals, and between them ran seedy back-streets complete with hookers and down-and-outs. And over this crime-ridden metropolis watched a Dark Knight who really was dark – a guy with serious psychological disturbances who tries to work them out by swooping round in black body armour and dishing out some hi-tech vigilante violence. This Batman's personal brand of justice is acted out with the aid of the sort of toys his wealthy alter ego Wayne could buy with his pocket change, including a new and suitably brooding-looking Batmobile[3] and an nicely under-lit Batcave.

The only thing that had the Bat-fans up in arms was the casting of Bruce Wayne/Batman. For the role, Burton chose Michael Keaton, best known for his work in light comedies like **Mr Mom** (1983), and who'd only recently graduated to a more outrageous role as the title spook in Burton's eccentric

ghost romp **Beetle Juice**. Keaton, the fans complained, wouldn't bring the required sense of *gravitas* to the role, and didn't have the required charisma. In the end, however, Keaton acquitted himself more than honourably as both Bruce Wayne and Batman, but the cries of the "DC Comics fundamentalists", as Keaton himself called them, would echo down as the big-screen Batman series continued. Once the film was released, though, their complaint changed slightly. Now the comic fans were joined by reviewers and the general public alike when they complained that, while Keaton's Batman was all well and good, he was blown off the screen by Jack Nicholson's portrayal of his arch-enemy, The Joker.

Dark fable though it may be – and one with a serious underlying message – **Batman** was designed as a summer blockbuster for the action-crazed, money-loving eighties, with the dual purpose of entertaining the public and making Warner Brothers a fortune. Which it did. In spite of a plot made rather disjointed by a writer's strike during the pre-production period, **Batman** grossed big, easily emerging as *the* summer movie of 1989, watched both by comic book fans and non-fans alike. Indeed, one of the ways in which it lured in the non-comic-buying public in was to cast as many big-name stars as possible, which is how Jack Nicholson ended up playing The Joker, and why Kim Basinger appeared as Vicky Vale, the sexy love-interest photo-reporter out to discover Batman's real identity[4].

Jack was actually cast first, before Keaton, and was one of the reasons that the producers decided to go with a name actor in the role of the Dark Knight, as opposed to an unknown (along the lines of Christopher Reeve in 1978's **Superman**). As Burton himself put it: "I kept imagining the reviews and hearing the response in my head, 'well, Jack's great, but the unknown so-and-so is nothing special!'"[5] However, while star power was a big part of it, Jack was also chosen because of his suitability to the role, something all concerned agreed on. Indeed, had they just wanted any big name, by that time Tom Cruise should have been fairly easy to woo away from **Days Of Thunder**. Nicholson did, after all, have something of a pedigree in playing homicidal maniacs in the likes of **The Shining** (1980), and the combination of his ability and larger-than-life star persona meant he'd be ideal for bringing an equally larger-than-life (although rather less well rewarded) cartoon character into reality. As Dann Gire describes it:

Nicholson juxtaposes unnerving jocularity with homicidal shenanigans, be it playfully puncturing a man's trachea or spraying face-melting acid from the flower on his lapel. Nicholson also cuts loose with the kind of ear-itating laugh that the joker might produce on the pages of a comic book, the kind of maniacal 'Ha! Ha! Ha! Ha!' scrawled over several panels in huge block letters that grow bigger as they cross the page.[6]

However, despite Batman creator Bob Kane's claims that Nicholson "is" The Joker (something he decided after seeing **The Shining**), and despite production designer Anton Furst's statements that neither he nor Burton would have felt the same about the film had Jack not taken the role, there were other actors under consideration. According to screenwriter Sam Hamm, Willem Dafoe looks just like The Joker, David Bowie would have been good because he's funny when he's sinister, and James Woods would have been a nice choice because he wouldn't have needed make-up. Ultimately, though, none of the above fitted the bill quite as Jack did, for the simple reason that while all may have had the acting ability (if slightly narrower smiles), they weren't all Names in the same way that Jack was. Jack provided the film with its perfect mixture of greater and lesser stars. Had any of these other actors been cast as The Joker, it's doubtful that Warner Brothers would have been able to get half as much free publicity out of the casting of Keaton as Batman. Keaton vs Dafoe/Woods/Bowie seems a far fairer match than Keaton vs Nicholson.

Or rather Nicholson vs Keaton. Right from the opening credits, in fact, it's fairly obvious that Nicholson is going to outshine his nemesis. Just as Marlon Brando had trumped Jack for first billing in **The Missouri Breaks**

(1976), here Nicholson trumps Keaton as the opening credits roll. And from there on in, the reasons why The Joker is way cooler than Batman become intrinsically linked to both the film's subtext and Nicholson's career pattern and persona.

It's been said that the typical Nicholson role includes much of the real-life Jack, as well as exhibiting strong traits of character duality. The Joker embodies both these elements, and plenty more. At the time of the film's release, *National Review* magazine described the Joker as "the ultimate Nicholson role, the performance he has been groping towards for two decades." And while on the surface, Jack and The Joker may not appear to have much in common beyond the fact that both are famous for their grins – Jack never having been seen in public with green hair and a Queen Elizabeth I-style white make-up job – in some ways, The Joker can be seen as a direct extension of Jack Nicholson, c. 1989, which is another of the reasons why he's so well-suited to the part. Just as Jack Nicholson – or the concept of him – is so much larger than life, so is everything about The Joker exaggerated, including that famous smile. And it takes an exaggerated person to bring to life something so over-the-top that it's unnerving, be it a smile or the state bureaucracy-gone-mad of Terry Gilliam's **Brazil** (1985).

It's not too difficult to tell that The Joker ain't smiling because he's happy. Like Pennywise, the evil clown in Stephen King's *It*, or Victor Hugo's *The Man Who Laughs*[7], the smile and the exaggerated laughter are hiding something. And what could be scarier than something you can't see? Especially if it's hidden by something that's apparently welcoming, like a smile or laughter – but not so welcoming that there isn't just a hint of the danger that lurks hidden in the depths. As Hugo himself puts it:

*Everything that is great has a sacred horror. It is easy to admire mediocrities and hills, but anything that is too high – a genius as well as a mountain, an assembly (of great men) as well as a masterpiece – is frightening when seen from too close.*[8]

So it is that too much of a good thing can be bad for you. And as to getting too close to The Joker (in ways other than just being in range of his acid-squirting button flower), more about that later. Again, however, it's unlikely that any of the other actors mentioned as potential Jokers would have had the presence to make the scary smile quite so scary as Jack does, and for one simple reason. Since Jack is far better known in his public persona as Mr. Hollywood, we're less likely to be threatened by him. Neither Woods, Dafoe, nor even Bowie are quite such high-profile Nice Guys, and they certainly aren't Nice Ordinary Guys. This is a status Jack has managed the amazing feat of maintaining despite the cash, the houses, the star status and the high-profile/highly volatile celebrity relationships with (among others) Anjelica Huston and Rebecca Broussard.

As befitting its blockbuster status, **Batman** was released amidst a storm of publicity and a merchandising bonanza the likes of which had rarely been seen before. Displaying great business savvy, Nicholson took a cut in salary in return for box office points and a chunk of the merchandising profits. At the end of the day, that meant he got to take home in the region of $60 million, which made him one of the highest-paid actors on the planet. But as Douglas Brode puts it, while other actors might have got the public's back up over the amount they were raking in, Nicholson was still seen as a likable Everyman "who takes his craft seriously and his image with a grain of salt".[9] As, indeed, does the Joker.

Even at the height of his counterculture days in the late sixties – rather like the man himself – Nicholson's characters could always be relied upon to display remarkable common sense. While flower power types lived by ideals alone, Stoney, Jack's hippy musician character in **Psych-Out** (1968) was in music not just for the love of it and the chance to communicate, but for the bread, man. While **Psych-Out** and **Batman** would first appear to be poles apart, closer examination would reveal they do have one thing in common – both were designed as money spinners, **Psych-Out** for exploitation schlock makers AIP and **Batman** for the oh-so-establishment WB. Indeed, from the days of his directorial debut **Drive, He Said** (1970) – a tale of draft-dodging and anarchy – through films like **One Flew Over The Cuckoo's Nest** (1975) and **Terms Of Endearment** (1983), Jack had seemingly become as mainstream an actor as it's possible to be, occupying – according to Brode again – the role of screen legend à la Humphrey Bogart or Spencer Tracy. But just as Stoney wanted to have his cake and eat it too, Jack went mainstream without selling out. Taking his cut of the tickets, T-shirts and action figures, Jack still has plenty of time on his way to the bank to cast a snickering backwards glance at the absurdity of a society that lets such things happen.

Just as Warner Bros. filled their studio store shelves with Batman pencil-sharpeners and bubble-bath, similarly, on-screen, The Joker hawks his Smylex toiletries to novelty-hungry Gothamites. Smylex toiletries are, of course, lethal in combination, and leave the corpse with the permanently etched ecstatic joker's grin of a happy consumer who's consumed just one novelty too many. In other words, they function in roughly the same way as the pointless paraphernalia churned out by the studios to cash in on their film[10]. These myriad commodities suggest that actual enjoyment of the film is secondary to the need to publicly broadcast the fact that one has actually seen it – a point to which countless frazzled parents coerced into buying both the model Batmobile and the Batcave Diorama (Figures Sold Separately) could doubtless relate.

Of course an awful lot of that paraphernalia *did* bear the Batman logo, one area in which the Dark Knight *did* seem to win out over The Joker, who didn't get *his* own logo. Or was the victory quite as clean cut as it seems? Talking about the discourses present in the film, Andrew Ross refers to "the ubiquitous Batman(TM) logo", circa July 1989, as "almost an alternate corporate logo for the swelling Warner Communications Group"[11]. It's pretty clear that the basic idea of what Batman is doing is Protecting Us From Evil, but in how twisted a manner? The Bat logo, according to Ross, is a symbol of the defence of white, aristocratic blood, but the Vampiric style of defence – perhaps not the best type.

Getting into his stride, later on in the film, the counter-cultural Joker goes ever further as he runs amok, trashing the paintings in an art gallery right before he takes over the city's Bicentennial parade, and, turning it into the ultimate parody, allows free (fake) cash to rain down on the people. "He's trying to kill me," says The Joker of Batman, almost breaking the fourth wall to do so. "I'm giving away free money. Who do you trust?" As such, the Joker is the sixties revolutionary grown up and wised up. He too mocks capitalism (and wears brightly-coloured clothes in the process), but he's smart enough to perpetrate his anarchy from within, having won over the people's trust through their own stupidity. Where the hippies harangued, The Joker insinuates, painting a clear picture of what's wrong and giving both the Gothamites and ourselves a working model of the corruption of the capitalist

system. "Look at the adoration I'm getting", he seems to be saying, "and the huge amounts of money, fame and success" (hardly ten minutes of the movie goes by without the Joker appearing onscreen on TV). "What kind of sick society allows this to happen and actually *enjoys* it?" But, as always, Jack/the Joker doesn't subscribe to simple, singular views, showing us both sides of the picture.

Just after the Joker's rampage through the art gallery, he corners Vicky Vale in the cafeteria, where she throws her glass of water over him. At the time, The Joker has a flesh-coloured face because he's wearing his "street make-up", but the water washes some off, revealing the chalk-white skin underneath. Even the racial viewpoint of the movie is skewed. According to Andrew Ross, "the Joker plays his role in whiteface, and sports an involuntary rictus grin that caricatures, along with his new, pathologically delirious personality, the old minstrel blackface routine of putting on a happy face."[12].The Joker also sells those Smylex toiletries which act on the skin, dances jerkily to the Prince soundtrack, and carries a boom box when trashing the museum. Clearly, it's not just the counter-culture white middle America has to worry about here, it's also, as Ross puts it, the "barbarians battering at the gates of western culture" (Ross, 31). But beyond that, it's clear that "we" (or at least our "guardian" Batman) *created* the problem that is The Joker, just as white attitudes initiated racial problems[13], and the fifties created the sixties. There's an even greater fear in play here than that of The

Joker turning up and killing us – the fear that, underneath, he's exactly the same as we are. There's a Joker lurking under the surface in all of us. But what does it take to bring him out?

The Joker was, of course, originally created by Batman himself. He starts out as plain Jack Napier (funny coincidence about the first name, huh?), a medium-powered hood who runs the show for master criminal Grissom (Jack Palance) and is having an affair with Grissom's moll Alicia (original supermodel Jerry Hall). Napier is fully convinced that Grissom knows nothing about this, but unfortunately, he's wrong, and Grissom sets him up to be busted by the police at an industrial plant. Batman turns up too, and in the ensuing shoot-out, allows Napier (seemingly by accident) to drop into a vat of acid, which bleaches his skin white and his hair green. Batman also plays an important part in creating the famous grin, when Napier's bullets bounce off his bulletproof cape and hit the crook in the face. Perhaps understandably, this sends The Joker soaring over the edge, and he turns from a cold-hearted, vain and seemingly imperturbable sharp-suited villain to a twirling, prancing, subversive maniac who describes himself as a "homicidal artist" and kills using (among other methods) a turbo-charged joke buzzer.

But if the Joker's a bona fide nutcase, with no agenda beyond creating havoc and taking over the city with a view to creating an even greater rumpus, Keaton's Batman is the flipside of chaos, representing the ultimate in character duality in the way he inversely reflects all the Joker's traits. Batman too, for example, was created by a great psychological disturbance – the death of his parents. He too lacks a specific agenda beyond the immediate gratification of offing expendable minor villains with the hazy eventual goal of cleaning up the city for good (exactly the opposite of the Joker's equally fuzzy plan, in other words). Both do what they do for obviously personal reasons as well: the Joker is a whirling dervish of a lunatic, hellbent on gaining revenge on the world. But Batman too is out for revenge on the criminal classes who murdered his parents. In the opening scene, when Batman apprehends two muggers who have just bashed a Nice Man over the head and stolen his wallet, Keaton doesn't do a Superman and check the victim's alright, he just contents himself with scaring the hell out of the bad guys and making sure they'll spread the message to all their lowlife friends. The psychological character duality between the pair is completed later when we find that not only did Batman create The Joker, but The Joker created Batman – or, at least, Jack Napier did, as he was the one who shot Mr and Mrs Wayne as they exited the theatre all those years ago.

This also takes the schema of the movie one step further. Anarchy and free love are not the answer to the establishment's staunch view of the world. In fact, they represent an extreme reaction, with its own inherent problems. The black and white vigilante form of crime busting Batman uses

is a reaction to the "ordinary" crime perpetrated by Napier, just as the garish super-crime methods used by The Joker are a reaction to Batman's hard-line approach. In the same way, the anarchic, turbulent sixties were a backlash against the conservative fifties, and the materialistic eighties a backlash against the poor-but-hippy values of the sixties.

But if **Easy Rider** failed to convert the world in 1969, it's pretty clear that nobody's going to listen now. Which is why, in the end, the Joker loses, just like the genre says he should, falling from Gotham cathedral and babbling hysterically at Batman about how "I created you, and then you say you created me...". In the end, Batman avenges his parents and can settle down to doing good in three more rather more moderate movies. For all its Vicky Vale Happy Meals, it turns out that social conventions are necessary because they keep things in order. Society just needs to learn not to get so obsessed with itself that it stifles free thought by going overboard about what's Right and Wrong, nor to get so drawn into images and periphery that it ignores the core. However much we might like to let out our inner Joker to trash whichever particular societal convention burns us up, it turns out to be not such a good idea after all. Since social conventions and the people who subscribe to them just won't learn, far better to rebel through the Joker on screen. It's safer.

Which brings things full circle. Why exactly is the Joker cooler than Batman? For the same reasons Jack Nicholson is cooler than Michael Keaton. The Joker does exactly what he wants, when he wants, he's smart and knowing. He's certainly smarter and more knowing than Batman, who sticks doggedly to the path of righteousness, without ever realising that it might not be all it's cracked up to be. Scriptwriter Hamm describes **Batman** as being about "a guy who has a sick hobby that fucks up his love life... it's like 'do I want to go out on a date and sleep with a woman, or do I want to put on my mask and cape and apprehend a couple of evil-doers?'"[14]. Above all, The Joker has fun with it and gets to enjoy his neuroses. Jack, meanwhile, gets to ridicule the system, make his point and bring home the bacon, which is, of course the sensible thing to do in his situation, even if he has to lose in the end. It's through The Joker that we get our vicarious pleasure while the movie's running, and it's through the dreams of what we'd do if we got billions of dollars for playing a comic strip bad guy that we get our kicks after we leave the cinema. And besides, who *wouldn't* kill for a million-dollar smile like that?

# NOTES

1. At the time the show went into production, network execs felt there was no way hip sixties types would take to a Batman played straight.

2. Robin did originally appear in Hamm's script, but was ejected because, as Hamm says "we had a pretty smooth story and we just couldn't get that bump in there. The duality we'd established in the character's (Batman's) make-up made it apparent that being Batman isn't very healthy. So it becomes sticky having Robin join in the crime-fighting scene and having it be seen as a positive kind of act." Robin did, of course, finally arrive in the shape of Chris O'Donnell in 1996's **Batman Forever**, opposite Big Screen Batman #2 Val Kilmer, where he was introduced using the device thought up to introduce him in **Batman**. One of a family troupe of acrobats, he joins forces with Batman after his family are killed by the bad guys. He went on to appear in 1997's critical and box-office failure **Batman And Robin**.

3. Anton Furst describes the Batmobile as "an extension of Batman's overall total look, meant to intimidate" (Jones, 58). Yet underneath the black curves of the car lurks the chassis of "America's Only Sports Car", the all-American Chevrolet Corvette. The sixties Batmobile was based on the Lincoln Futura showcar. How's that for the darkness and the duality of the American Dream?

4. Vale was originally to be played as a brunette by Sean Young, until she broke her leg. The most obvious legacy of the writer's strike evident in the film is in the way that after spending half the movie trying to find out who Batman is, when butler Alfred reveals the truth to her, Vale doesn't even react.

5. Jones, Alan: "Directing The Legend", "Designing The Legend" and "Batman: Tim Burton Interview", *Cinefantastique*, 20, n1-2, November 1989:52.

6. Gire, Dann, "Rating The Legend" *Cinefantastique* 20, n1-2, November 1989:50.

7. *L'Homme Qui Rit (The Man Who Laughs)*, filmed in 1928 by Paul Leni, tells the story of a nobleman whose face is carved into a permanent smile by the king after his father is killed for treachery, he becomes a fairground attraction, falls in love with a blind girl and is lured into evil by the King's jester, much of which directly parallels events pertaining to The Joker in *Batman*. Bob Kane has claimed Hugo's story as the original inspiration for The Joker. See also William Castle's grotesque masterpiece, **Mr. Sardonicus** (1961), another telling of the same story.

8. Hugo, Victor *Ninety-Three, Book Three,* T. Nelson & Sons, NY: 1910.

9. Brode, Douglas *The Films Of Jack Nicholson;* Citadel, 1996:96.

10. Owning the merchandise became seriously obsessive, to the point that you had to have the "right" merchandise. In the summer of 1989, aged 13, I went to see **Batman** with a friend. We both wore black and yellow bat-logo T-shirts, but much to his consternation, mine had a "TM" logo underneath, defining it as a Warner Bros. official product, while his didn't, designating it a knock-off. The general consensus was that mine was the superior, even though for all practical purposes, both were identical.

11.  Ross, Andrew "Ballots, Bullets Or Batmen: Can Cultural Studies Do The Right Thing?" *Screen* 31:1, Spring 1990:26.

12.  Ross, 1990:31.

13.  The Joker may seem to represent "black", but we all know who gets the black outfit, and the Joker is a white man under extra-white make-up, just to add a few more layers.

14.  Rebello, Stephen "Sam Hamm Interview", *Cinefantastique*, 20, n1-2, November 1989:45.

# JACK AT THE CROSSING: 'THE CROSSING GUARD'

The commercial and critical "failure" of Sean Penn's **The Crossing Guard** (1995) has overshadowed the significance of Jack Nicholson's performance. Although Dennis Bingham regards the actor's '80s and '90s roles as an example of how "stars who begin with internal criticism of the dominant order are eventually disciplined and constrained by ideology, by the soothing balms of money and success"[1], **The Crossing Guard** is much more than an isolated contradiction of the above statement. Nicholson's involvement is a major collaborative contribution to a film experimenting with Sean Penn's adaptation of John Cassavetes's cinematic legacy, Nicholson's dialectical use of two screen acting traditions, and a star's embodiment of ageing masculinity.

Like his Hollywood neighbour, Marlon Brando, Jack Nicholson seems to have abandoned the radical acting innovations of his earlier screen career by settling for big bucks and cute, non-challenging roles in films such as **The Witches Of Eastwick, Broadcast News** (both 1987), **Batman** (1989), **Mars Attacks** (1996) and **As Good As It Gets** (1997). However, unlike Brando, whose work with Coppola and Bertolucci embody his last significant acting performances, Nicholson has not entirely limited himself to lazy, "walk-on" roles, cameos, and supporting performances. **Ironweed** (1987), **The Two Jakes** (1990), and **Hoffa** (1992) appear as personal projects appealing to the actor in terms of themes involving ageing, parental failure, regret for the past, and betrayal of radical ideals. These films complemented Nicholson's earlier star signification as a "thirty-something" casualty of the American Dream in **Five Easy Pieces** (1970), **Carnal Knowledge** (1971), **The King Of Marvin Gardens** (1972) and **The Last Detail** (1973). In **The Crossing Guard**, Nicholson appears as an older world-weary version of a character delivering the opening monologue from **The King Of Marvin Gardens**, as well as one approaching the end of a sexual blind alley begun in the closing scenes of **Carnal Knowledge**.

**The Crossing Guard** sees Nicholson return to his earlier cinematic goal of "pushing at the modern edges of acting".[2] It reveals once more his interest in "introducing advances in post-war theatre to Hollywood film".[3] This evokes the '60s era of American cinema when many of his contemporaries attempted to bring devices from European and independent film into the system. Richard Dyer's classic axiom concerning stars reflecting contradictions within their contemporary social eras[4] is relevant to Jack Nicholson's role in **The Crossing Guard**. Nicholson now appears at the crossroads of his cinematic career. No longer young, he is ageing like Marlon

Brando in **Last Tango In Paris** (1972). But his character still suffers the same type of masculine crisis characterizing his early performances. **The Crossing Guard** displays the actor as an older man, in physical decline, attempting to act out the role of a vengeful father which he believes he has to do. However, like Brando's Kurtz in **Apocalypse Now** (1979), Nicholson's Freddy Gale is clearly a "hollow man". **The Crossing Guard** is also deliberately allusive and demanding. It calls on audiences to work at elucidating meaning in a quasi-Godardian cinematic manner. The film also eschews the conformist visual style and linearity of contemporary Hollywood to engage in an ambiguity characteristic of one of Sean Penn's major influences, John Cassavetes. Like Cassavetes, Penn opposes traditional Hollywood conventions by mostly eliminating establishing shots, point-of-view shots, traditional dramatic arcs within scenes, classical shot-reverse-shot structures punctuated by concisely written meaningful sentences, and conventional use of music. Furthermore, as Cassavetes, Penn interrogates the features of everyday "performance" and the social "faces" people must put on for their daily survival, faces often psychologically destructive for those wearing them. Both Viggo Mortensen in **The Indian Runner** (1991) and Jack Nicholson in **The Crossing Guard** represent psychologically damaged victims of this process.[5] Secondly, like **The Indian Runner**, **The Crossing Guard** deliberately avoids traditional generic expectations to arrive at a novel and redemptive ending. Penn disavows the **Death Wish** formula whereby an ageing patriarch such as Charles Bronson would execute the scumbag responsible for his daughter's death. Instead, **The Crossing Guard** examines the psychological victims of an emotional American wasteland. Avenger Freddy and proposed victim John Booth are psychological twins suffering from similar personal dilemmas involving guilt and the attempt to recover coherent identity.

As well as utilizing motifs common to both American literature (*Moby Dick*) and Hollywood cinema (**The Searchers**), **The Crossing Guard** also rejects that debilitating "regeneration through violence" syndrome that has plagued American culture from its very beginning[6]. It chooses instead a redemptive ending similar to that brief reconciliation between hunter and quarry in Larry Cohen's **It's Alive** (1973). While Cohen's climactic reunion is only temporary before patriarchal social forces again disruptively intervene, **The Crossing Guard** concludes with its two characters still alive. They both engage in mutual reconciliation and mourning as a new dawn breaks out over the Los Angeles horizon. As Marlon Brando recognized, it is one of the most emotionally touching moments in a contemporary cinema now a cultural wasteland.

Like Penn's unjustly neglected **The Indian Runner**, **The Crossing Guard** is cinematically over-ambitious. But it is also another of the director's imaginative apprentice works which Trevor Johnston sees as suggesting that "the future of a personal American cinema may not be as dark as it sometimes seems".[7] Despite the resemblance of Freddy Gale's pursuit of John Booth to that classic cinematic archetype embodied by **The Searchers** (1956), Penn's treatment is far more developed and mature than earlier "move brat" renditions such as Martin Scorsese's **Taxi Driver** (1975) and Paul Schrader's **Hardcore** (1978). John Booth represents Freddy's version of Joseph Conrad's "The Secret Sharer". He not only challenges Freddy's insecure male masquerade but also makes him confront his personal demons. Although the film's conclusion may resemble those dangerous seductive levels of contemporary patriarchal remasculinization criticized by Susan Jeffords and Tania Modleski[8], **The Crossing Guard** operates on a more mature level. Jack Nicholson's acting forms an important part of this process.

Nicholson's performance eclectically combines two screen acting traditions associated with Stanislavsky and Delsarte. The first aims to create an honest and "realist" performance style. It teaches actors to emote internally and create characters by relying upon memory and emotion. The second style is more emphatic. It involves the expressive displayal of gesture and exaggerated performance.[9] These two styles often appear throughout Nicholson's acting career. In 1986, Ron Rosenbaum recognized that Nicholson was not an instinctual actor. His performance style never drew upon spontaneity or improvisation. Nicholson had demonstrated to Rosenbaum a particular type of vocal exercise involving tonal variations of the same short phrase based upon Method acting techniques taught him by teachers such as Martin Landau and Jeff Corey. Rosenbaum commented, "This is a man who still analyzes his roles in terms of Stanislavskian 'polarities'; who, during those lean years, would sit around Los Angeles coffee houses for hours discussing Stanislavskian metaphysics..."[10] Quoting both Albert Camus and Anton Chekhov, Nicholson reflected upon the absurdity of life and the actor's mission involving the subversion of conventional wisdom. Rosenbaum believed Nicholson's star persona operated most effectively in films such as **Terms Of Endearment** (1983), **Carnal Knowledge, Five Easy Pieces, Reds** (1981), **The Shining** (1980), and **The Passenger** (1975). These works often featured Nicholson's character undergoing painful contradictions between illusion and reality.

Nicholson's performance in **The Crossing Guard** also represents his acting version of Pudovkin's conception of film editing. Pudovkin compared editing to a process of "building bricks" to produce a particular structural meaning.[11] In Nicholson's case, his performance involves returning to the roots of his acting interests by reinvoking ideas that stimulated the actor and his generation three decades ago. Nicholson's performance draws upon, in an autumnal mode, that existentialist angst associated with the summer of his BBS production days. No longer young, he is now older, but still no wiser than his earlier characters. As Bingham comments, "Such films put a spectator in the position of flattering masochism; the characters bear little responsibility for their actions. Like Meursault in Camus's *L'Etranger*, they are motiveless, doomed, and stripped of control by existence itself."[12] Ironically, although Freddy believes he has a goal, his actions towards are really contradictory and indicative of repressed doubt. He is really a "lost soul" attempting to perform a masculine role at odds with the alienated and masochistic dimensions of his real personality.

Nicholson's performance in **The Crossing Guard** represents an important "brick" in a Pudovkin tradition of acting influenced by Stanislavsky. His role once more employs acting devices which Bingham sees characteristic of the star's better performances, namely a Brechtian "spectacle of masculinism as a set of assumptions about mastery and superiority".[13] **The Crossing Guard** sees Jack return to the traditions of younger days, but now embodied in an older physique. He also employs his own version of Brecht's *gestus*, namely involving the performative aspects of bodily posture, accent, and facial expression to exemplify a particular social relationship. In **The Crossing Guard**, this involves the impossibility of performing a socially expected, violent, male role. Nicholson thus combines Stanislavsky and Brechtian traditions.

Actor and director knowingly collaborate in utilizing earlier traditions and adapting them to their version of a new independent cinema of the '90s. **The Crossing Guard** draws upon Cassavetes's films such as **Faces** (1968), **Husbands** (1970, **A Woman Under The Influence** (1974), and **The Killing Of A Chinese Bookie** (1976) to rework them in specific ways. Like John Marley and Lynn Carlin in **Faces**, Nicholson's Freddy Gale desperately performs an agonized masquerade. He collapses under the strain like Gena Rowlands in **A Woman Under The Influence** (1974) and attempts a role at odds with his own desires like Ben Gazzara in **The Killing Of A Chinese Bookie**.

**The Crossing Guard** opens with the visually evocative slow-motion shot of a flame passing over the unclothed body of a night-club dancer. It becomes juxtaposed with scenes of a rap group attempting to articulate the trauma of coping with surviving the death of a family member killed by drunk driving. This image introduces conflicting tensions of pain and control affecting Freddy himself. Emotionally devastated survivor, Bobby (John Savage) articulates his fears of letting people near him. He also experiences nightmares of losing anyone he allows to penetrate his emotional armour. Nightclub scenes reveal Freddy amidst a group of drinking buddies voyeuristically eyeing strippers and complicitly enjoying sexist jokes. Performance ritual is not just confined to the stage. Freddy also performs a role as much as the women he ogles and beds to quell his insecure sense of masculinity. During sequences which alternatively move from night club to rap group, Bobby speaks of psychic disembodiment following the death of his older brother. "I miss me. Where's Bobby?" This line follows the night club image of a dancer stroking her breast with a knife in imagery both sadistic and masochistic. Watched intently by Freddy's ex-wife, Mary (Anjelica Huston), Bobby's dilemma contains revealing insights into Freddy's condition. Both involve denial and emptiness. This receives visual emphasis in slow-motion shots depicting Freddy walking through the crowded Los Angeles streets like a sleepwalker. Bubbles float over Freddy suggesting the ephemeral nature of his own dream world. The poignant lyrics of Bruce Springsteen's appropriately titled song, "Missing" occur. Its key lines are "Last night I dreamed the sky went black/Drifting down could not get back/Lost in trouble and so far from home/She was missing, missing..."

The opening two sequences visually articulate the duality structuring the film. As well as having two symbiotic characters, **The Crossing Guard** also employs several repeating motifs such as the two jeweller shops Freddy passes to reach his own, two graveyard scenes, and two appearances of the street singer first seen in the opening slow-motion sequence.

These scenes suggest that Freddy's male world of sadism and control contains hidden masochistic dimensions harmful to human development. Like Travis Bickle of **Taxi Driver** (1975), Freddy is also "God's lonely man" living in a harmfully solipsistic world. But he will undergo a physical and personal existential odyssey when he finally "returns home" to come to terms with the death of his daughter. Until then, he does not wish to confront the personal demons within his psyche. Unlike Herman Melville's Captain Ahab, Freddy encounters his demonized "Moby Dick" offering personal redemption.

Springsteen's song not only refers to Freddy missing his daughter, Emily, killed by drunk driver John Booth but also his own "missing" status. Freddy dwells in existential alienation and absurdity. He beds women young enough to be his daughters, pathetically attempting substitutions for his lost emotional paternal relationship. The repeated lines of "Missing" emphasizes mirror imagery Penn employs to link Freddy with John Booth (David Morse)[14] Penn uses Morse's character as a catalyst. But, unlike his figure in **The Indian Runner** who causes the psychological destruction of his Viet Nam veteran brother (Viggo Mortensen) by forcing him into a dangerous world of normality, Morse now performs a more redemptive function. The audience first sees Booth on his last day in prison as he looks at his face in the mirror. Two alternating rapid flashbacks occur. They show him masochistically punishing himself for his crime by banging his head on the cell bars during an earlier time in prison. Although Booth never repeats this action, his explicit rage acts as an inverse parallel to that harmfully repressed masochism existing within Freddy concealed under a sadistically vengeful veneer. Freddy's hidden

feelings display themselves in opposing modes of behaviour. He performs the aggressive roles of voyeur and lecherous Casanova which his age and declining physique render ludicrous. The film's first "morning after" scene reveals an aged Freddy, whose sagging breasts almost match those of his evening conquest. As Freud shows, sadism and masochism are alternating instinctual forces within the human personality which mirror each other and often evoke contradictory modes of behaviour.[15] They are also dangerous forces active today in western society.[16] Whether conscious or not, the film's directing and performance styles recognize this. But, unlike Freud's pessimistic attitudes and retrogressive capitulation to a supposedly monolithic concept of "human nature", **The Crossing Guard** suggests a way out of this dilemma.

Nicholson's performance style embodies these two psychological patterns by combining Method technique with the Delsarte expressive style of **Goin' South** (1978) and **The Shining**. Method technique generally dominates Nicholson's performance while Delsarte gestures operate in a "return of the repressed" manner. This latter process appears whenever Freddy finds himself in situation which questions his chosen role of sexually aggressive male and vengeful father. Nicholson's performative relationship to Anjelica Huston in their second teaming since **Prizzi's Honor** (1985) draws upon the Method's "affective memory" concept Nicholson employed in **Five Easy Pieces**. Brando claimed also claimed this influenced his monologues in **Last Tango In Paris** (1972). Scenes between Freddy and his ex-wife Mary, now re-married after the death of their daughter in a car accident, evoke the real-life relationship of these stars as well as behavioral patterns influencing their fictional surrogates. Jack/Freddy and Anjelica/Mary exhibit character tensions ranging from hostility, sympathy, and physical aggression. On one level, Huston's performance draws upon the real life pain of abandonment and betrayal which she faced after the breakdown of her romantic relationship with Nicholson. On the fictional level, these tensions represent antagonism between a father who loved his deceased daughter "not too wisely but too well" and a wife who pities a husband who became weak and "small" after the accident. While Freddy exists in his own repressed personal hell, Mary attempts to suppress painful memories by changing her personal life and marrying again. However, like Freddy, she also explodes physically. This occurs when she violently pushes Roger (Robbie Robertson) away from comforting her after Freddy suddenly returns to her home. Personal and theatrical levels coincide. The fictional relationship also parallels the frequent phenomenon of couples divorcing after the traumatic death of a child.

Freddy exists in an emotional wasteland performing a self-appointed role of tough, hard-boiled, avenging male businessman. He perfunctorily beds stripper after stripper, ignores the one woman (Priscilla Barnes) who feels genuine warmth towards him, and acts like a man in control. But he is not. When Freddy breaks his promise to Mary by telling her of Booth's release from prison, Nicholson changes from subdued Method acting into a Delsarte technique reminiscent of his Jack Torrance in **The Shining** as he holds Roger in an incongruous wrestler "bear hold". (Ironically, Booth briefly performs this gesture upon Jo-Jo in their last meeting later in the film.) Freddy also intervenes in a argument between his gay shop assistant and a demanding customer (Eileen Ryan). He angrily explodes at her and forgets his controlled "manager" role. His outburst appears stimulated by the woman's demeaning comment about his assistant's sexuality. It also queries Freddy's presumed masculinity by questioning his reasons for employing such a person. When Mary finally attempts to reach out to him in the diner, her comment, "I pity you. I don't know how to help you," triggers off Freddy's masculine rage and a renewed desire to execute Booth (i.e. "A man's gotta do what a man's gotta do"). Freddy has previously phoned her and broke down weeping like a helpless child needing a mother as he confessed his nightmare of seeing John Booth as a crossing guard when Freddy kills his own daughter like a drunken driver. This is the first occasion in the film where Nicholson uses the "affective memory" emotional technique seen in **Five Easy Pieces**. It will finally occur in the climactic graveyard scene.

Although Freddy wishes to perform a "manly" role, he is really pathetic and insecure. As an ageing male leering at young female bodies and an avenger who not only stumbles across the entrance to Booth's trailer but forgets to load his gun, his masculine performance is ludicrous. Freddy really masochistically punishes himself by refusing to recognize the finality of his daughter's death. He conceals these feelings under a sadistic male guise. However, Booth already accepts his guilt and wishes to perform the role of a "crossing guard" for Freddy. He also recognizes the different, but equally harmful, emotional state affecting his adversary. Booth initially suggests Freddy wait three days before their next encounter. Although Booth places himself in a dangerous position, he never envisages becoming a "sacrificial victim", as Penn visually suggests by having a boat named *Aztec* pass him one morning. By reaching out to Freddy, Booth attempts a healing role. Although Booth has long accepted responsibility for causing the accident five years before, he still feels uneasy at the way prison life has allowed him to come to terms with the situation. But, as his attempted relationship with Jo-Jo (Robin Wright) reveals, he still labours under a debilitating burden of guilt. He decides to become a redemptive crossing guard by forcing his adversary to face his repressed pain and accept the death of a beloved daughter which he continually denies.

Ironically, the police later arrest Freddy as a drunken driver. But he escapes, still determined to perform his masculine role. When he finds Booth holding a rifle on him, Freddy darkly comments upon the "poetic justice" of his new situation as well as his expressing determination to fulfil his self-appointed role. "I'm going to give you a laugh kid. I just got pulled up tonight, the whole bit, drunken driving... I'm on the run. I'm on your property with a gun. I figure you can shoot me and get away clean. So, I'm going to get my gun... and I swear I'm going to kill you." The following shots alternately zoom-in on Booth and Freddy. Two intercut close-ups of their eyes then occur. Booth's hesitates in pulling the trigger, drops his rifle, and runs away pursued by Freddy. After Freddy wounds Booth, the latter collapses as a torrent of water runs over him, a scene filmed in slow-motion. Generally associated with Freddy, this is the last time this effect appears in the film. It leads to the climactic movement where avenging father and perpetrator become "born again". Both men begin to recognize their spiritual kinship. A close-up of Freddy's eyes suggests his growing awareness. Booth recovers and leads Freddy to his daughter's grave. He speaks to the headstone, "Daddy's Coming. He needs your help." Freddy sees the gravestone for the first time. He recognizes the difference between his dark fantasies and the reality he has to confront, finally. He gives Booth his gun, holds out his hand to his former quarry. Freddy breaks into tears for the second and last time in the film. He acknowledges his repressed personal pain and an awareness of his real vulnerable self. It is a powerful climactic moment – and Jack Nicholson's finest performance of the decade.

**The Crossing Guard** is a film dependent upon Jack Nicholson's powerful performance techniques. Evoking that lost alternative tradition of American cinema acting, Nicholson's outstanding performance employs radical acting techniques now sadly absent from the screen. Although Jack Nicholson may now be associated with the multi-million dollar Hollywood establishment and films which never really stretch his creative talents, **The Crossing Guard** remains the one exception, in an extremely depressing decade for American cinema, where star and director attempt to suggest a way forward.

# NOTES

1.  Dennis Bingham, *Acting Male: Masculinities In The Films Of James Stewart, Jack Nicholson, And Clint Eastwood* (New Jersey: Rutgers University Press, 1994), 159.

2.  Jaimie Wolf, "It's All Right Jack", *American Film*, 9.4 (1984):36.

3.  Bingham, 103.

4.  Richard Dyer, *Stars* (London: British Film Institute, 1979).

5.  I wish to acknowledge the insights of Mike Robins in an e-mail discussion of Sean Penn's work.

6.  See here, Richard Slotkin, *Regeneration Through Violence: The Mythology Of The American Frontier 1600-1860* (Middletown, Conn.: Wesleyan University Press, 1973); *The Fatal Environment: The Myth Of Custer And The Age Of Industrialization 1800-1890* (New York: Athenaeum, 1985); and *Gunfighter Nation: The Myth Of The Frontier In Twentieth Century America* (New York: Atheneum, 1992).

7.  Trevor Johnston, **"The Crossing Guard"**, *Sight And Sound* 6.9 (1996):37. See also Tony Williams, **"The Indian Runner"**, *Vietnam War Films*. Eds. Jean-Jacques Malo and Tony Williams (Jefferson, N.C.: McFarland & Co, 1994), 211-212.

8.  See Susan Jeffords, *The Remasculinization Of America: Gender And The Vietnam War* (Bloomington: Indiana University Press, 1989); "Can Masculinity Be Terminated?" *Screening The Male: Exploring Masculinities In Hollywood Cinema*. Eds. Steven Cohan and Ina Rae Hark (New York: Routledge, 1993), 245-262; Tania Modleski, *Feminism Without Women: Culture And Criticism In A "Post-Feminist" Age* (New York: Routledge, 1991).

9.  For a detailed description of both techniques see James Naremore, *Acting In The Cinema* (Berkeley: University of California Press, 1988), 192-212 (demonstrated in detail by Marlon Brando's performance in **On The Waterfront**), 52-67.

10. See Ron Rosenbaum, "Acting: The Creative Mind Of Jack Nicholson", *New York Times Magazine*, 13 July 1986:12. For Nicholson's eclectic approach see Bingham, 116. According to Nicholson's first teacher, Jeff Corey, the type of instruction he gave as a teacher involved elements of Delsarte, Brecht, Peter Brook, and the Stanislavsky tradition interpreted by Lee Strasberg. See Patrick McGilligan, "Corey-graphy", *Film Comment* 25.6 (1989):38. Naremore associates Nicholson with *both* naturalist and method acting techniques. See Naremore, *Acting*, 45n, 198, and 203, the last quoting Nicholson's interview with Rosenbaum where he confessed that his traumatic weeping scene was based upon Method acting's "affective memory". At least two similar scenes occur in **The Crossing Guard**.

11. Rosenbaum, 49, quotes Stanley Kubrick's acclaim of Nicholson's performance in **The Shining** as one involving an actor bringing "great intelligence" to his role. Kubrick has also acclaimed Pudovkin's techniques. See Thomas Allen Nelson, *Kubrick: Inside A Film Artist's Maze* (Bloomington, Indiana University Press), 8-13, 18-19.

12. Bingham, 105.

13. Bingham, 102.

14. The occurrences are too frequent to mention in this study. However, it is significant that the two sons from Freddy and Anjelica's marriage are also twins.

15. Sigmund Freud, "Instincts And Their Vicissitudes", *On Metapsychology: The Theory Of Psychoanalysis. The Pelican Freud Library. Volume 11* (London: Penguin, 1984), 105-38.

16. See Lynn S. Chancer, *Sadomasochism In Everyday Life: The Dynamics Of Power And Powerlessness* (New Brunswick: Rutgers University Press, 1992).

# A JACK NICHOLSON FILMOGRAPHY

**The Cry Baby Killer** (1958)
**The Wild Ride** (1960)
**The Little Shop Of Horrors** (1960)
**Too Soon To Love** (1960)
**The Broken Land** (1962)
**Studs Lonigan** (1962)
**The Terror** (1962)
**The Raven** (1962)
**Back Door To Hell** (1964)
**Ensign Pulver** (1964)
**Ride In The Whirlwind** (1965)
**The Shooting** (1965)
**Flight To Fury** (1966)
**Hells Angels On Wheels** (1967)
**The St Valentines Day Massacre**
　　(uncredited, 1967)
**Psych-Out** (1968)
**Head** (uncredited, 1968)
**Easy Rider** (1969)
**The Rebel Rousers** (1970)
**On A Clear Day You Can See**
　　**Forever** (1970)
**Five Easy Pieces** (1970)
**A Safe Place** (1971)
**Carnal Knowledge** (1971)
**The King Of Marvin Gardens**
　　(1972)
**The Last Detail** (1973)
**Chinatown** (1974)
**The Passenger** (1975)
**Tommy** (1975)
**The Fortune** (1975)
**One Flew Over The Cuckoo's Nest**
　　(1975)
**The Last Tycoon** (1976)
**The Missouri Breaks** (1976)

**Goin' South** (1978)
**The Shining** (1980)
**Notre Dame de la Croisette** (1981)
**The Postman Always Rings Twice**
　　(1981)
**Reds** (1981)
**The Border** (1982)
**Terms Of Endearment** (1983)
**Prizzi's Honor** (1985)
**Heartburn** (1986)
**The Witches Of Eastwick** (1987)
**Ironweed** (1987)
**Broadcast News** (1987)
**Batman** (1989)
**The Two Jakes** (1990)
**A Few Good Men** (1992)
**Man Trouble** (1992)
**Hoffa** (1992)
**Wolf** (1994)
**The Crossing Guard** (1995)
**The Evening Star** (1996)
**Mars Attacks!** (1996)
**Blood And Wine** (1997)
**As Good As It Gets** (1997)

# INDEX OF FILMS

*Page number in bold indicates an illustration*